The End of Religion
& Other Writings

Essays and Interviews on
Religion, Interreligious Dialogue,
& Jewish Renewal
1999-2019

Netanel Miles-Yépez

CHARIS MANDALA
Des Moines, New Mexico
2023

Contemplative Life,
Embodied Spirituality
& Sacred Activism

Charis Mandala Publishing
P. O. Box 21295
Boulder, CO 80308
charisinterspirituality.org

Design and composition by Charis Mandala Publishing.
Cover design by Charis Mandala Publishing
Cover art of "The (Great) Tower of Babel" by Pieter Bruegel the Elder, Oil on Wood Panel, ca. 1563

ISBN: 978-1-960360-00-7 (Hardcover)
ISBN: 978-1-960360-01-4 (Paperback)

Manufactured in the United States of America

Praise for *The End of Religion and Other Writings* . . .

"Pir Netanel Miles-Yépez' latest book is a ground-breaking addition to the discourse on spirituality and its significance in shaping our future. As conventional religious establishments continue to lose their relevance, Miles-Yépez is at the forefront of a movement that is redefining the role of religion in contemporary society. His innovative ideas and profound insights are not only inspiring, but also transformative, providing a new outlook on spirituality that can serve as a roadmap for our future. This book is essential reading for anyone seeking a more profound comprehension of spirituality and its capacity to guide us through the complexities of our era."

> — Rev. Adam Bucko, co-founder of The Center for Spiritual Imagination, author of *Let Your Heartbreak Be Your Guide,* and co-author of *The New Monasticism*

"Part restless visionary, part tender heart, Netanel Miles-Yépez engagingly shares his vigorous and sometimes playful interrogation of the prophetic and the contemplative. This little book of essays will intrigue and challenge you, making you want to first call a friend for a coffeeshop conversation. Then you will both want to jump up and join the enduring dance of the vitality of the human spirit."

> — Dr. Judith Simmer-Brown, Distinguished Professor Emeritx at Naropa University, author of *Dakini's Warm Breath,* and co-editor of *Meditation and the Classroom*

"If you are ready for a deeply engaging and always delightful discussion about what it means to be religious and spiritual today, this is the book for you. "Religion as we have known it is breaking down," Netanel Miles-Yépez observes with startling clarity. Where do we go from here if we long for spiritual transformation and religious engagement? Miles-Yépez, a brilliant scholar and open-hearted spiritual practitioner, guides us through a profound journey towards a shared spiritual future by addressing issues ranging from interreligious dialogue to Hasidic renewal, to the paradox of the pursuit of happiness."

— Dr. Anna Sun, Associate Professor of Religious Studies and Sociology at Duke University, author of *Confucianism as a World Religion*, co-author of *Against Happiness*, and editor of *Situating Spirituality*.

"Netanel's grasp of my music and writing over the years has been a special thing for me as an artist and a human. At a time when the internet was ramping up with opinions and I was feeling alone in a sea of misunderstanding, Netanel sailed into my life with an understanding of my songs that was refreshing. He continued over the years to be the only writer that I felt was understanding my music at its depth. Having deep knowledge of the worlds that I was traveling, he could often tell the seed from which the song sprouted. Having a deep understanding of the human spirit, he was able to see where my soul was swimming."

— Matisyahu, hip-hop and reggae artist, whose albums include *Spark Seeker* and *Akeda*

"Whether he's grappling with the purpose of religion, or abuses of it, the rise of interspirituality or Jewish Renewal, or discussing the rewards of interspiritual dialogue with renowned spiritual leaders, or simply sharing his own experiences, with Netanel Miles-Yépez you know you are in good hands. You want to follow his clear, crisp prose, his insightful questions and probing mind, and his honest self-reflection wherever they lead you. This is a wonderful book for seekers of all faiths and paths. By putting spirituality above dogma and creed, it serves as a bright light for those who long for the real, and are open to truth wherever they find it in our increasingly multicultural and interconnected world."

— Alejandra Warden, author of *Remembrance: A Vision of the Sacred Feminine and the Renewal of the Earth*

To my dear friends
Adam Bucko & Rory McEntee

As a part of the Charis Foundation for New Monasticism & Interspirituality, Charis Mandala Publishing is dedicated to the emergence of contemplative spirituality in all areas of life. As one of Charis Foundation's strategic array of programs and partnerships, we endeavor to serve a broad-based movement of interspiritually-oriented new monasticism. As a publisher of both fiction and non-fiction works that draw on the world's great contemplative traditions, Charis Mandala Publishing crosses boundaries between philosophy, theology, spiritual teachings, art, poetry, and novels.

'Charis' is the ancient Greek word for 'grace,' while 'Mandala' is the Sanskrit word for 'circle,' symbolizing wholeness and awakening. Thus, in the spirit of interspirituality, Charis Mandala represents a 'Circle of Grace,' one that supports an embodied spirituality for practitioners of all types—whether "spiritual but not religious" or members of traditional religious paths—in their desire for a committed contemplative life that remains connected to the world and its needs through sacred activism.

To learn more about the Charis Foundation please visit us at charisinterspirituality.org.

CONTENTS

Part IV
Problems and Perspectives
on the Spiritual Path

Acknowledgements

Among those to be thanked are first and foremost my dear friends, Father Adam Bucko and Dr. Rory McEntee, to whom this book is dedicated, and who, from 2012 to the present, have been the chief appreciators of many of these essays (especially those of the first and third sections), often urging me to publish them in a small book through the years.

Most of this work was written while my beloved teacher, Rabbi Zalman Schachter-Shalomi, *z"l* ('Reb Zalman,' 1924-2014), was still alive, and thus feels very personal and bound up with our relationship. If there is anything good here, it should be understood that Reb Zalman's profound generosity was a part of making it possible.

So, too, none of this work would have been possible without the love and friendship of my former wife, Jennifer E.C. Phares, who witnessed and supported the slow growth-cycle of the man who wrote these things. She was a special appreciator of "Matisyahu and the New T'shuvah," which is here re-published.

Special thanks is also due to my friend and colleague Dr. Edward Bastian who, at Reb Zalman's suggestion, hired me to be the "Editor of Print and Website Publishing" for the Spiritual Paths Foundation in 2002. It is he who brought me into relationship with Father Thomas Keating,

Swami Atmarupananda, Tania Leontov, and the rest of the Snowmass Conference members.

Thank you to my friend, Matisyahu Miller—the musical artist Matisyahu—with whom I came into relationship after he first read my article "Matisyahu and the New T'shuvah," appreciating my view of his music and the unique difficulties he faced as an artist in those years. This led to our collaboration on an article for *The Huffington Post*, "The Ḥanukkah Miracle of Re-Dedication," which was timed to release with his new Ḥanukkah song, the proceeds of which would benefit people impacted by Hurricane Sandy. Later, I would write official album descriptions for his albums *Akeda* (2014) and *Live at Stubb's Vol. III* (2015).

I would also like to express my gratitude to and affection for a number of important people in my life during the period in which these essays were written: Edward W. Bastian, Tessa Bielecki, Gavin Breeze, Bahir Davis, David Denny, Leigh Ann Dillinger, Carol Dionisio, Michael Gregory, Zvi Ish-Shalom, Jason Jesurum Jay, Michael and Ruth Gan Kagan, Yogi Nataraja Kallio, Sam Krezinski, Brett and Abigail Larson, Bradford and Gerra Lewis, Zachary Amitai Malone, Jonathan McDowell, James Meadows, Nicholas Phares, Raj Seymour, Kal Sigmond and Sari Shore, Rebecca Sipos, and Robbie Tesar.

Friends of today who should also be mentioned include: Sara Sorche Berry, Lasette Brown, Lisa Chatham, Allison DeHart, Timothy Holbert, Ramon Parish, David Rome, Or Rose, Judith Simmer-Brown, Christopher "Gabriel" Steadman, Alejandra Warden, Carson Warden, Anna Wolfe, and Greg Yamada.

Acknowledgments

I would also like to thank the students in my "Religion and Mystical Experience" and "Interspiritual Dialogue" courses at Naropa University (2016-2023) who have read some of these essays, as well as my colleagues in the Department of Wisdom Traditions: Amelia Hall, Nataraja Kallio, Giovannina Jobson, Phil Stanley, Ben Williams, and Stephanie Yuhas. Likewise, I am indebted to President Charles Lief for his continual support.

As always, I would like to thank my extended family in the Yesod Foundation—Aaron Claman, Tirzah Firestone, David Friedman, Thomas Hast, Bobbie Zelkind—as well as Eve Ilsen, for their continued friendship and support through the years. I would also like to thank my more recent colleagues at the Fetzer Institute—Bob Boisture, Dan Cardinali, Bill Vendley, Michelle Scheidt, Xiaoan Li, Shakiyla Smith, Nathan Moore, Sarah Roelofs, Rylee Prach, Lauren Lott, and particularly Meghan Campbell—conversations with whom have prompted me to think of collecting these essays in this book.

A special thanks to my beloved support and partner, Jamelah N. Zidan, who makes so much possible; and to Master's of Divinity student, Rachel Fryke, who generously read over the manuscript and made many good suggestions and necessary corrections.

— N.M-Y.

Preface

SOON AFTER I published the title essay of this collection in *The Huffington Post* (in March of 2014), I received a series of angry responses from readers who evidently felt I had tricked and betrayed them. Based on the title, "The End of Religion," they had expected to find a devastating critique—another version of Sam Harris' *The End of Faith*—providing them with a little more ammunition for what they already believed (or wanted to be true) concerning religion. And I was counting on that. Not that I had any desire to 'trick' them; but I was well aware that it was a provocative title that would attract attention.

The essay itself was part of a personal experiment: I wanted to see if I could present my more sophisticated thoughts on religion and spirituality in an accessible form that could be easily understood, without appealing to the abstruse academic language in which I had been trained. I have always found religion in all its manifestations fascinating, and have always believed that it could be interesting and teachable to general readers, if presented in a manner that demonstrates what is *actually* interesting about it.

It also seemed like a responsibility, as it is abundantly clear that religion is *not* well understood in our society, either by those who generally embrace it, or by those who vehemently oppose it. Thus, the provocative title "The End of Religion," and the immediate interest it garnered—both from those who objected, and those who wished it to be so—was *itself* a demonstration of a point: we seek proof for what we *already* believe, error in what we *already* oppose, and only rarely seek to understand what we do not.

However, this was only an afterthought. The truth is, I had been in love with the title long before I ever made it my own. When I was a young History of Religions student at Michigan State University, my mentor, Dr. Alford T. Welch, an excellent 'old-school' scholar and expert in Qur'anic Studies, introduced me to the work of Wilfred Cantwell Smith and his little book *The Meaning and End of Religion* (1962). The title captured me immediately, just as I had hoped it would capture my readers years later. Reading the title for the first time, I delighted in witnessing my own momentary confusion at the sight of the word "End," and the sudden realization that 'end' also means 'purpose!' Thus, the first sentence and opening question of Smith's book, "What is religion, or *a* religion?"[1]

I had been thinking about the 'purpose of religion,' consciously or unconsciously, ever since. Thus, the title "The End of Religion" was not really meant to be clever, opportunistic or sensational, but genuinely indicative of my own interest and aim: I wanted to talk about the 'end' or 'purpose' of religion, to rescue it from misunderstanding, to explore and redefine it in some helpful manner, because we need to as a society.

Thus, the double-*entendre* I actually intended was between the "end" or purpose of religion, and the actual end of "an old and outworn idea of religion as *an-end-in-*

itself, as an idol that has—for far too long—been mistaken for its maker and its goal."

But, as it is almost impossible to discuss 'religion' today without it being treated as something opposed to 'spirituality,' at least in liberal circles, it also seemed necessary to look at the relationship between the two, and to explore the future of each. Thus, the three essays— "The End of Religion," "Spiritual *and* Religious," and "The Religion of Spirituality"—form an unfolding series, each building on the other.

Preceding these essays in this volume is another short essay on a related subject, "Epochs and Reality Maps," exploring the phenomenon of paradigm shift in our belief systems. This essay is the oldest material in this collection, being written in 1999 while I was still a graduate student at the Naropa Institute in Boulder, Colorado. Part of my master's thesis, it was later included as a chapter in my book with Rabbi Zalman Schachter-Shalomi, *God Hidden, Whereabouts Unknown* (2013).

Together, these four essays comprise Part I of the book, and set the contextual tone for everything that follows.

From 2002 to 2014, I worked closely with the founder of the Spiritual Paths Institute, Dr. Edward Bastian. A Buddhist scholar and member of the famous Snowmass Interreligious Conference, Ed hired me to work for the institute and brought me into contact with the other members of the Snowmass Conference. Indeed, it was at his suggestion in 2004 that I was asked to work on a book about the Snowmass Conference, for which I interviewed all of the current members, and some of its past members, too.

In this way, part of my early career was defined by the publication of the book *The Common Heart: An Experience of Interreligious Dialogue* (2006), the work of dialogue in general, and my connections to the Snowmass Conference. Indeed, even today, my foundation—Charis Foundation for New Monasticism & Interspirituality—continues the work and dialogical legacy of the original Snowmass Conference in its Charis Snowmass Dialogues and Charis Circles.

For this reason, Part II of this collection reflects my own thoughts about the Snowmass Conference and my personal contacts with some of these remarkable individuals, through a series of published interviews with three of them—Father Thomas Keating, who would become a special mentor to me, Swami Atmarupananda, and Tania Leontov.

In "Paradigms of Ecumenical Dialogue as a Spiritual Practice" (originally published in *The Journal of Ecumenical Studies*, Winter 2008) I explore the notion that dialogue might become an adjunct spiritual practice to our historical religious traditions, an idea which later grew into the conviction that dialogue *itself* is the primary spiritual practice of interspirituality.

Part III of this collection reflects the other major concern of these years of my life, my work articulating a "Fourth Turning of Hasidism" with Rabbi Zalman Schachter-Shalomi, *z"l*, my *rebbe*, with whom I wrote several books, including *A Heart Afire: Stories and Teachings of the Early Hasidic Masters* (2009) and *A Hidden Light: Stories and Teachings of Early ḤaBaD and Bratzlav Hasidism* (2011). Together, we dialogued for more than a decade on the subject of a *new* Hasidism; but as he neared the end of his life, we still had no definitive expression of that dialogue. Thus, just before he died, I decided to write a kind of manifesto, "Foundations of a Fourth Turning of Hasidism," as a gift for him. I gave a type-set copy to him in the hospital the last time I saw him.

Another aspect of our dialogue on Hasidism concerned spiritual guides and spiritual guidance in the Hasidic tradition, represented here in "A Rebbe's Soul, A Hasid's Yearning," a dialogue between us published in his book *Geologist of the Soul: Talks on Rebbe-craft and Spiritual Leadership* (2012).

Added to these are two essays which marked a new direction in my own evolving thought on Jewish Renewal (the movement founded by my *rebbe),* a view that I called 'Essentialist Judaism.' These are "Matisyahu & The New T'shuvah" on art and identity in the Jewish community, and "The Miracle of Re-Dedication" (written with the aforementioned musician, Matisyahu), looking at the Jewish holiday of Ḥannukah from an inner prespective that makes it symbolically relevant to all spiritual seekers.

Part IV of this collection includes two essays that represent more personal reflections written in this period. "The Other Side of Fear," originally written for (but not actually included in) Dr. Jim Sharon's collection *Ordinary Men, Extraordinary Lives: Defining Moments* (2013), was published instead in my journal *Spectrum* (2013), and was later recommended by the Registrar to incoming students at Naropa University for its description of the school and its values. "What's Happiness Got to Do with It?" is a brief personal reflection written immediately after receiving a phone call from a struggling student seeking spiritual help and guidance. It is the most recent material included in this collection, being written in 2018, a particularly difficult year in my life.

The last piece included in this section, and the last piece in the book, is an interview with me by my former student Zachary Amitai Malone on "The Uses and Abuses of Religion and Spiritual Leadership Today." Though conducted in 2012, its wide-ranging content reflects much of the other material in the book, and thus serves as an appropriate 'bookend' for everything that precedes it.

Re-reading all of these essays and interviews today, I find that there are many things that I would not say in quite the same manner now; but I also feel that the entire collection (while not inclusive of all that I wrote in these years) is still very representative of my thinking and who I was in that period, and I do not feel inclined to betray who I was then by disavowing him now. There is much that I am proud of here, a little that I find slightly embarrassing, and some things that I hope will be of value to you.

— NETANEL MILES-YÉPEZ
   BOULDER, COLORADO
   JULY 5TH, 2023

PART I
Religion & Spirituality

Epochs & Reality Maps*

AN EPOCH IS a new beginning, a fluid period of transition, establishing 'new gods' for a new era. In the long history of consciousness, the human community has experienced many such epochs, significant periods of change in the general character of our awareness.

In these liquid moments of vague beginning, a sleeper awakens. The sleeper is not one human being, but a feeling of discontent seeded through an entire generation, or a series of generations. Their 'waking-up' is gradual— light flooding through the eyelids, an awareness of time and need causing a general stir through the body. It does not happen in a single moment; it is a waking-sequence progressing from the slow and blunted awareness experienced at first light to the deft precision and clear head of mid-morning. But the discontented of that epochal period awaken to more than an empty belly; they also find they have a longing and taste for something they have never before experienced.

The epoch occurs when the efficacy of the then dominant 'reality map'[1]—that inherited system of shared

---

* Written between 1999 and 2000, this essay on paradigm shift was first published in *Spectrum: A Journal of Renewal Spirituality* (Vol. 2; No. 1, 2006) as a section of the longer essay on the kabbalistic concept of *tzimtzum*, "God Hidden, Whereabouts Unknown."

religious and cultural beliefs by which we orient ourselves in all situations—begins to break down, initiating a process of shifting from one paradigm to another, more viable, and better able to sustain its constituents in a new situation.

The epochal period is simply a natural, adaptive, evolutionary process for ensuring our collective survival. It is a tool for reshaping the landscape of our collective mental and spiritual frontiers, creating a new reality map to replace the one that preceded it.

The new reality map is a "guide for the perplexed," as well as a contemporary container for the *magisterium*, or collected knowledge of a tradition. It is a kind of oracle to which the spiritual seeker can bring their confusion—it listens, understands, and tells them, *'This is how it is; this is as it should be,'* and the seeker is comforted.

But it is also a container for ideas whose shape represents but a stage of development in the whole history of ideas. It speaks to a particular world-situation, to the culture of the time, and it is in accord with the knowledge of the day. It is timely, and thus can easily handle questions from the world-view of which it is a part. But it is not exclusive to the exact moment in history which gave birth to it either; it is built with some 'give' in its sides, so that it can grow with the people it serves.

And yet, as with every time-born thing, a moment comes when the container has stretched to the breaking-point and bursts, loosing once again the primal-flow. The cycle is completed and one returns to the epochal period.

Of course, this is an abstracted and intellectual way of talking about the process of paradigm shift. Most people experience the 'death throes' and 'birth pangs' of the shifting process as difficult and painful. For when a reality map ceases to function and serve the needs of its constituents, they quite naturally feel betrayed by it. After all, bringing their most profound feelings and questions to it, they are met with what seem like mere platitudes. Asking for the *'all'* that it once provided to those who went before them, they receive barely enough to fill their mouths.

But the answers they are getting are *not* mere platitudes, as they seem; they are just the answers of *another time,* another situation, another paradigm. For the reality map they are addressing was built to address the needs of others, long ago. What was once responsive and innovative is now clumsy, struggling even to understand the questions being asked of it. The Copernican Revolution could not have been conceived by the Ptolemaic reality map that came before it. Thus, the generation living at the end of a paradigm reaches out to its reality map, seeking a genuine response, and is disappointed to receive what seems like a condescending recapitulation of tired 'truths' and answers from the 'good old days.' The situation is untenable, and the utter frustration of it is what eventually gives rise to the dynamic period of conception between paradigms.

Thus, the failure to communicate with a new generation drives the creative flow to conceive of a new and more responsive reality map; the tragedy of the 'communication gap' turns out to be but the birth pangs of a new paradigm, the catalyst for a spiritual revolution. As the boundary-pushing artist Robert Irwin put it, "Revolutions don't cause change; change causes revolutions."[2]

These epochal days are precisely those "interesting times" in which the old Chinese curse wishes you to live; that is to say—*full of difficulties.* For even though it will be clear to some that the old paradigm has become irrelevant, its influence will live on in others, others who will hold all the more tightly to it, precisely because of all the changes in their world.

In the epochal period, the body of the slouched and breathless king has not yet yielded the throne; but nor has a clear successor emerged to clear away the ruined body and its influence. One is reminded of Finnegan in Joyce's *Finnegans Wake*, who himself represents a passing paradigm. After suffering a bad fall while drunk, his comrades think he is dead and decide to hold an Irish wake for him. Of course, he is not dead, but merely unconscious, and soon rises from his coffin during the festivities, only to be held down by his reveling friends who insist that he "rest in peace," seeing as his successor has already arrived to replace him!

So the way ahead often seems blocked by the unyielding 'dead weight' of the past. And yet, things are not as hopeless or as static as they seem. For the old 'king' is dying, and the land is being saturated with a new and creative vitality from his 'body.' Just as humus is the life of the soil, the decaying body of the old king, the old reality map, gives impetus to its emerging successor. At that moment, a ferment of syncretistic-creation suddenly arises, guided by a teleological pull toward a new paradigm. It is a period of radical experimentation and rich cross-fertilization; the *empirical-experiential* is raised above the *legal-rational*, and the once rigid forms become fluid again, opening tradition to revitalizing influences. The memory of the old is re-interpreted and elaborated to suit the needs of a new age, a new spiritual landscape. In this way, another reality map is born.

"The Tower" by artist Pamela Coleman Smith for
The Rider-Waite Tarot Deck, 1909.

The End of Religion*

RELIGION AS WE have known it is breaking down. The evidence is everywhere we look. It is in the despicable rhetoric and violence of politically-oriented religious extremists, far and near. It is in the scandals and abuses plaguing our ecclesiastical structures. It is in the surface-tension between the 'religious right' and modern culture, in the growing indifference of that culture to religion, and its occasional disgust with it.

And yet, as I see it, it is not religion *itself* that is so evidently coming apart in these examples; it is an old and outworn idea of religion as *an-end-in-itself,* as an idol that has—for far too long—been mistaken for its maker and its goal. It is that idol which is now being broken. Religion itself will go on; it is how we relate to it that will change, and must change, if we are to reclaim its genuine usefulness to us.

Over a century ago, the Russian philosopher, P. D. Ouspensky explored the symbolism of "The Tower" —a card in the *major arcana* of the Tarot deck—as a metaphor for religion. The tower, he said, was begun in a time before memory, as a monument to the sacred, as a reminder of the true tower which exists in each one of

---

* Originally published in *The Huffington Post,* March 3rd, 2014, this is the first in a three-part series of experimental articles written for popular consumption to expand our understanding of religion, spirituality, and their unfolding.

us, its every level representing a level to be climbed on the inside. But even before the foundations were fully laid, the builders of the tower began to *"believe in the tower of stone"* they were building, and to teach others to believe in it, too. To them, the tower was itself sacred, and soon they tried to control access to all its doors and windows, and to occupy the summit, and the very 'rights to heaven' as they saw it. They even began to fight over these 'rights' in their confusion. Thus, of all the people of the earth, the worshippers of the tower were the most surprised when heaven spoke from beyond its walls in the form of a lightning bolt, striking the summit, sending its priests sprawling to the ground, where they lay helpless amid the rubble. Now, all who look upon the tower and its ruin, and see its fallen priests and broken summit—open unto heaven, as it always should have been—*know* not to believe in the tower.[1]

As the metaphor suggests, the real issue is one of remembering the original function of the tower, of maintaining one's awareness of the true meaning and purpose of religion, i.e., that it is a reminder of the sacred. The problem is, it is just so easy for us to forget that religion is not itself sacred, but merely a vessel for the sacred. Although, truth be told, I wonder how many people ever made that distinction in the first place.

I do not think I would be going out on a limb to say that religion is not well understood in our culture. Often, it is assumed to be 'right and necessary' by the religious, or 'backward and unnecessary' by the secular; but how many people really know anything about religion in itself, about its function or how it works? How many people, whether religious or secular, can actually give a working definition of religion? Perhaps if we knew something about its true end and purpose, we might better understand why religion as we have known it is breaking down, and more importantly, get a glimpse of what is now evolving—namely, *'the religion of spirituality.'* But let me back up a step and propose a working definition of religion:

> *Religion is a sociological construct meant to take us back to the primary experience from which it arose; it enshrines an ideal and provides one with a structured approach to spiritual awakening or transformation.*

That is to say, religion is what follows in the wake of the spiritual luminary's breakthrough experience; it is what happens *after* Muhammad receives the revelation, or the awakening of the Buddha; it is what their disciples cobble together from reports of those experiences, using them to make a 'map' to lead themselves and others back to the source experience. As the Buddha himself taught: religion is like a raft one makes and uses to cross a river; once you are on the other side, you needn't carry it around on your back.[2] It is a means to an end, not the end itself.

We must always remember then that the map is not the sacred territory; it must be used by us (with its original purpose in mind) and not the other way around. As my teacher, Zalman Schachter-Shalomi, once put it (while commenting on the abuses of various religious extremists in a Yom Kippur sermon), *"Good religion* puts itself in the service of God; *bad religion* puts God in the service of religion."[3]

It is the latter paradigm that usually has us so upset with religion—that causes us to question its foundations—and which is the cause of all that seems to be breaking down in religion. But this is religion *misused* and *misconstrued.* It is a false religion that puts the sacred in its own service. False religion is to true religion as the cancerous cell is to the healthy cell. It is this imposter that provokes our most vehement objections, and which now has us looking up at a broken tower and boldly declaring, 'A new day for spirituality!' and waving goodbye to the 'old-time religion.'

Spiritual and Religious*

WITHOUT A DOUBT, it is a new day for spirituality. In the popularity contest of modern life, it is religion which 'can't get a date for the prom.' More and more, people are declaring themselves *"spiritual-but-not-religious,"* which represents both progress and a problem for us.

The problem with being 'spiritual-but-not-religious' is that it is a dead-end for the spiritual seeker. Without the positive 'tools' of religion, it can only describe a person's point of view—on the one hand, a sense of wonder and personal conviction about transcendent possibilities and the *numinous;* on the other, a disinterest in, or dissatisfaction with known religious history, structures, and dogmas.

Don't get me wrong; I'm not criticizing people who identify as 'spiritual-but-not-religious.' Anybody who feels compelled to choose spirituality over religion has, in my opinion, "chosen the better part"—to quote Jesus from the Gospels.[1] Sometimes it seems like the only appropriate response to the religious confusion of our time. The problem arises when we are asked, or ask ourselves, *"How* are you spiritual-but-not-religious?" For when we try to answer the question, we either have a difficult time

---

* Originally published in *The Huffington Post,* March 3rd, 2014, this is the second in a three-part series of experimental articles written for popular consumption to expand our understanding of religion, spirituality, and their unfolding.

explaining it, or immediately start to name activities or refer to teachings from existing religious traditions that actually undermine the original statement.

This is because it is actually a mistake to separate religion and spirituality, as if the two were opposed to one another. The truth is that they are natural partners and cannot be separated without doing damage to the greater goal. Religion in this partnership is what you *do* or *use* to accomplish spiritual transformation. It is not something in which you must *believe*. It is a tool that performs a service for us, something we utilize for our own spiritual development. Unfortunately, too often, we find ourselves being used by the tool; but that is not the fault of religion.

It is up to us to gain an understanding of what it is with which we are dealing, to know what our own position is relative to our religious traditions. Obviously, if we make an idol out of religion, we become its servant and can expect to be used. But if religion is the tool that we use to gain access to the sacred, then we are in the right relative position to achieve our own ends with it.

For as long as we can remember, we have been in relationship with this thing called 'religion.' So long in fact that we sometimes forget who created whom. We treat it like an 'All-Knowing God' over our lives, slavishly trying to live up to its apparently 'divine' dictates. The irony is, we created it to help us remember how to connect with the sacred, to help us achieve an experience of the ultimate reality. Even the word tells us as much; for 'religion' derives from the Latin *re-ligare*, meaning 'to link back' or 're-connect.' It is what links us to the source or essence of our being, to all that we would remember about how to connect with that source or essence.

When discussing his theory of paradigm shift and spiritual renewal, the always innovative Zalman Schachter-Shalomi would sometimes borrow the Latin word *magisterium* from Catholicism to describe a religion's collected body of knowledge or wisdom.[2] But it is also a good way to think about religion in general, i.e., as a body of spiritual teachings and lore, rituals and techniques, carried down and growing ever-larger through the centuries, like a slow-moving glacier carried onward by its own weight and inertia. That is to say, religion is our collective memory of spiritual technologies and instruction manuals, the means by which we can 're-connect' with the sacred dimension—but which is not itself sacred.

What *is* sacred is spirit or spirituality. Spirit is the living essence of the sacred, the divine life, as it were. *Spiritus*, as the Latin suggests, is the divine 'breath' in the body of the human being, the planet, and the universe. It is the 'active ingredient' in all things, including religion. If I were to concretize it into a working definition based on human experience, it might be characterized thus:

> *Spirituality is an awareness of a transcendent value encompassing, permeating, or hiding just below the surface of material existence; it is the living essence of the sacred at the center of one's life.*

Nevertheless, spirit is impotent without a body to carry its essential message. And this is the rub for the 'spiritual-but-not-religious.' While religion without spirituality is, as so many have come to realize, like a body without a soul or the animating spark of life; at the same time, spirituality without religion is a soul without a body—it cannot *do* anything in the world. Thus, one's spirituality is limited to a vague sense of something 'other,' something 'beyond,' which may bring us hope, but little help. Without structures of teaching and practice, i.e., religion, we cannot accomplish the spiritual transformation of our lives for which so many of us long.

Still, the idea of being 'spiritual-but-not-religious' is a critical insight for us today. What we are really saying is that we have a sense that the two—*spirituality* and *religion*— have become divorced, that the life-spirit has left the body of religion, making it dead for us. When people began to quote Nietzsche in the late 1960s, saying, "God is dead!"[3] what many actually meant was that religion was dead for them. But even if we acknowledge the 'death of religion,' we are still left with the problem of the soul without a body. This is where so many of us find ourselves today, longing for spirituality, but lacking the means of deepening our relationship with it. Although spirituality is indeed "the better part," it is limited in what it can do for us unless we learn to pair it with a proper understanding of religion.

The Religion of Spirituality*

IN 1949, MAX ZELLER, a disciple of the visionary psychotherapist Carl Jung, came to Jung with a dream he could not understand. In the dream, he saw a "temple of vast dimensions" under construction. As far as he could see, in every direction, there were multitudes of people participating in the building of the temple. Though the temple was only in its beginning stages, the foundation had already been laid, and he was himself working on a pillar. Hearing this, Jung simply nodded and said, "this is the temple we are all building today." It is *the new religion.* We don't know all the builders, of course, because they are "in India and China and in Russia, and all over the world," but "this new religion *will* come together."[1]

This is what Jung believed. The problem for us is that the process has only just begun, and we do not yet know what shape it will take or how it can help us.

Looking at the rubble of the past and the chaotic building-site of the present, many people today—both spiritually-inclined and secular—are understandably declaring 'the end of religion.' But what neither seems to understand is that religion cannot die unless we, as

---

* Originally published in *The Huffington Post*, August 12th, 2014, this is the third in a three-part series of experimental articles written for popular consumption to expand our understanding of religion, spirituality, and their unfolding.

human beings, somehow cease to feel and long for that indefinable, ineffable awareness of the sacred to which religion is merely a response. Until that happens, we will continue to reach out to the sacred, and we will use religion to get it.

The real question is, what kind of religion will we use to access the sacred? Will we continue to use the old religions of the past, whether in their conventional or mystical forms? Will we evolve and participate in new hyphenated fusions of traditions like Christian-Zen or Sufi-Hasidism? Or will we embrace a greater religion of spirituality, as some are already suggesting? I think the simple answer is, 'Yes.'

Until fairly late in the 20th-century, no matter where you might find yourself on the map, you were likely to live in a more or less homogenous culture, where most people were 'like you' in language, race, and religion. If you knew anything about another religion, you probably viewed it as something strange or inferior. But today, we live in a world where cultures are increasingly bumping up against one another, and where religions must co-exist.

Today, we find that our neighbors are Hindu, and our co-workers Muslim. In almost every metropolitan area, we have access to Yoga classes, Buddhist meditation, Hindu satsangs, Muslim Sufi zikrs, Christian Centering Prayer groups, and Jewish Renewal services. Living in this spiritual marketplace, in a time when many of us find ourselves cut-off from the religions of our birth, and with almost every religious possibility within reach, some are asking, 'How do we choose between them?' And yet, my sense is that this is not actually the question they want to ask; I think they are bewildered at having to make a choice at all . . . Indeed, I don't think they *want* to choose anymore.

In the Jewish mystical tradition, the expulsion from Eden is characterized as the loss of the primal unity. Having eaten the fruit of the *eitz ha-da'at*, the 'tree of knowledge,' humanity suddenly found itself cast headlong into the world of separation, into a world devoid of the sacred, in which we could only see the differences between things.[2] But in the last century, we have again eaten the fruit of the tree of knowledge—of other cultures and religions—and found, paradoxically, that we are really one people, one body, whose needs are the concern of all.

Our current access to all the religions of the planet is slowly (or perhaps quickly) putting an end to the myth of religious superiority, the view we call 'triumphalism.' But something else is happing as well. It is also eroding the clearly definable boundaries of our current religions, giving many of us the feeling that there is no longer any particular reason to be exclusively wedded to one religion or another. Many people no longer want to be boxed-in to any one tradition. Having had access to them all, and having seen the unique tools and beauty of each, who can believe that any one of them has all the answers anymore?

Given this awareness, which religion you choose really becomes a matter of emphasis and individual need. For a tall person, a ladder with rungs far apart is preferable, while a shorter person obviously prefers one with rungs set closer together. Still, both are ladders, and both are designed to facilitate access to higher regions. In the same way, religions have all developed the same *basic tools* to deliver an experience of the sacred; but each has a different emphasis and uses these tools in different ways, just as the ladder is used for different jobs. What the spiritual seeker is able to do today, which is different than through most of our past, is *choose* which religion (or even which aspect of a religion) is most suitable to their needs, their purpose, and their abilities.

In the transition from the 20th to the 21st-century, the gradual dawning of this awareness of personal choice has led to an interesting evolutionary phenomenon, one I like to call, 'hyphenated spirituality.'[3] With all the jostling and bumping up against one another that happens in the universe, new relationships are bound to form, just as atoms gain and lose electrons, or different chemical compounds are formed in seemingly random interactions. In the world of religion, such interactions have led to the development of hyphenated loyalties— Christian priests who have become recognized Zen roshis or Vedanta swamis, rabbis who have become Sufi shaykhs or embraced a more shamanic form of Judaism.

Today, there is hardly anyone who doesn't have some kind of 'hyphen,' whether they be dedicated Christians devoted to Jungian psychology or resolved atheists with a deeply enriching Yoga practice, couples learning to handle the demands of inter-marriage or individuals integrating dual cultural identities. So why should it be any different with religions?

Although there is certainly an element of choice at work here, it is also clearly an evolutionary process, the planet mashing things together, as it always has, creating new forms of life and a healthy diversity for itself.

But this phenomenon of hyphenated religion is just the beginning of a larger process. Each hyphen must, in time, join to form a part of the mortise-and-tenon construction of 'the temple of the new religion,' described in the dream of Jung's disciple. In this process, the *magisterium*—the body of spiritual teachings, lore, rituals and techniques— of each individual religion must, in the interaction with other religious traditions, begin to 'surrender electrons' and form a new *magisterium* that "transcends and includes" both.[4] The process will go on, contributing to and eventually forming a greater *magisterium* of all religions, where the myths and practices of each will become the rightful inheritance of all people. In this sense, it will be a true religion of humanity, though I believe it will be defined as a 'religion of spirituality,' with these basic values:

> *The religion of spirituality will recognize the centrality of the spiritual, valuing it above religion, which must serve exclusively as a cultivator of spiritual awareness. The religion of spirituality will be comprised of the* magisteria *of all religions and unified by the primordial* mysterium *at the heart of all. It will recognize the call of the spirit as the source of all previous religions, and will utilize the deep structures of religion, made clear by comparative analysis, as the catalyzing basis for further spiritual evolution. The distinctively nuanced teachings and practices of independently developed* magisteria *will continue to serve the needs of individuals and their unique spiritual orientations from within the greater, unified* magisterium *of the religion of spirituality.*

Why is "the new religion" to be defined by spirituality? Because the 'spiritual-but-not-religious' have declared it so. They have made it clear that spirituality is more important than religion. What they have not yet discovered is what to *do* about it; for *doing* is the territory of religion.

Religion is the tool that allows us to access the spirit with regularity, to catalyze growth and spiritual maturity, to accomplish spiritual awakening and transformation. Thus, religion in the future must be the handmaiden of spirituality. Though both are essential ingredients, one is clearly the servant of the other. Over time, these two ingredients—the deep structures of religion and the heart-essence of spirituality—will be extracted from the individual religions, making a religion not of the Buddha or the Christ, not of the mind or the heart, but of Humanity and Wholeness, the parts and nuances of each the inheritance of all, a reflection of the primordial human archetype, *Adam Kadmon,* as it is called in the Jewish mystical tradition.

This is my conviction. But it is also clear to me that we are not there yet, and will not be for a very long time. It is not enough to have a vision of the future and theoretical access to the 'Greater *Magisterium* of the Religion of Spirituality.' We must also understand those deeper structures of religion, the basic technology of how religion works to accomplish spiritual transformation, and put that understanding into practice over a long period of experimentation.

Actual understanding will come slowly, organically. We are only beginning to understand what it means to have commitments in more than one tradition. We still don't have a firm grasp on how one balances and honors each without making one or both anemic. And what will be the role of the historical traditions in a universal structure which must, over time, make them all less relevant, or at least relative? How painful will the descent into a lesser degree of relevance be, and how will we deal with the inevitable reactions of violence which we are already witnessing? Our questions still far outnumber our answers.

After Jung had interpreted the dream of the temple of "the new religion," his student, Zeller, asked him if he knew how long it would take to build.

Jung answered without hesitation, "About six hundred years."

"Where do you know this from?" Zeller asked.

"From other people's dreams and from my own."[5]

Did Jung mean, six hundred years in transition to the new religion, or six hundred years for that religion to reach its peak? And what does it mean that the foundation has already been laid? However we interpret the dream, three things are clear: our current religions will continue for a long time yet; they will evolve and begin to hyphenate; and the great experiment of the religion of spirituality will proceed, slowly creating the structures of spiritual practice that will define it as a true incubator for spiritual transformation. For this is what is lacking today, and it is the reason we must bear with the slow evolutionary process.

PART II

The Snowmass Conference
& Interreligious Dialogue

The Snowmass Conference
& the True Heart of Dialogue*

THERE IS A COMMON misconception about the purpose of interreligious dialogue. Often, assuming that purpose to be 'instruction,' or an exercise in 'comparative religion,' well-intentioned participants sometimes prepare in advance, looking for similarities and differences in their traditions, hoping to find arcane bits of information with which to make an impression on the other. But this is to miss the point, albeit subtly. For the subject is not really 'religion' at all, but a *relationship* based on dialogue.

It is not wrong to prepare for a dialogue, of course; but it is a mistake to think that a dialogue between, say, two representatives of different religious traditions, is really about two *religions,* rather than the relationship of two individuals with different religious commitments. Though it is, admittedly, a subtle distinction, it is precisely this emphasis on relationship that made the dialogue of the Snowmass Interreligious Conference (often simply, the Snowmass Conference) such a unique and inspiring phenomenon in the world of religion.

* This article was first published in Himayat Inayati's *Awakenings: The Newsletter of Universal Awakening* (November 2006), and later republished in *Spectrum: A Journal of Renewal Spirituality* (Vol. 2; No. 1, 2006).

The Snowmass Interreligious Conference was originally the idea of Father Thomas Keating, one of the pioneers of interreligious dialogue in the Christian tradition and co-founder of the highly influential Centering Prayer movement. Having resigned as abbot of St. Joseph's Abbey (a Cistercian monastery in Spencer, Massachusetts) in 1981, Father Thomas then took up residence at St. Benedict's Monastery in Snowmass, Colorado. Officially retired, he began to devote his time to the dialogue work he loved.

In 1983, he was invited to participate in a series Buddhist-Christian dialogues at the Naropa Institute in Boulder, Colorado, that would ultimately change his whole approach to dialogue. During these sessions, Father Thomas noticed something interesting:

> I noticed that we, the dialoguers, weren't speaking to one another so much as we were addressing the audience. But, on the two occasions when the conveners succeeded in bringing us together a day before the conference, we got on very well and actually got to talk to one another as peers, albeit all too briefly. So I asked myself, what would happen if the whole point was just to get together and talk, without an audience? And what if it was broader than just a Buddhist–Christian dialogue?[1]

The next year, after collecting a host of personal recommendations, he issued special invitations to a private retreat for a small group of spiritual teachers from the world's great religious traditions. Among them were: Ani Pema Chödrön, Dr. Douglas Steere, Srimata Gayatri

Devi, Grandfather Gerald Red Elk, Rabbi Rami Shapiro, Bernie Glassman Sensei, and Imam Bilal Hyde. It was as impressive a roster as any public interreligious dialogue had ever had, except that this dialogue was to take place far from any cameras or eager spectators, in an isolated little monastery in the Rocky Mountains. These teachers (and a few others) would be the attendees of the first Snowmass Conference at St. Benedict's Monastery.

Naturally, on the first day the group talked about the unique nature of the meeting. Everyone understood the significance of meeting in private, but many were still unsure of how to go about the dialogue in this atmosphere. What were they to talk about? And at what level of exchange were they expected to speak?

Father Thomas knew that if this dialogue was going to be successful, it would have to be based on intimacy. But this was a group of strangers. It was obvious that they needed to tell their stories to one another first; comparative religion would have to wait. "This was the reason we were disinclined to have any observers at the Snowmass Conference," Father Thomas told me, "because what was developing was a kind of friendship that enabled us to feel comfortable and safe enough to share, to disclose to each other, what our own spiritual journey was like . . . You usually won't tell your secrets to somebody unless you're friends or until you know that person. So the idea of getting acquainted and being at ease in private was a primary goal."[2]

But even if the space was safe enough in terms of privacy, there was still one question in the back of their minds: should the conversations be recorded? It was clear that this was an historic meeting, and some wondered if they had an obligation to record the sessions:

> When the question was raised, "Do we want to tape some of this?" Grandfather Gerald Red Elk said, "No, that would not be good, because then we would be hesitant about people back home hearing what we say. This is intimate stuff, and I think we should not share it outside the group. If the wisdom needs to be heard, it will be heard." That won the favor of everyone, and we've never taped a conference . . .[3]

Thus began one of the oldest and longest-running interreligious dialogues in the world, and certainly one of the most unique. Over the years, word leaked-out about this unusual cabal, and with it came many invitations to hold their dialogue in a public setting. On the occasions that they acquiesced (mostly in the early years) it was an unmitigated disappointment for all of them. The public loved it, but the members felt that something was missing. So they declined any further invitations and went back to what they loved best, an intimate dialogue among friends.

This they continued for twenty years, weathering changes in membership, sickness, deaths, and the increasing fame of some of their members. In 2004, acknowledging their 20th anniversary, they began to wonder if perhaps they had served their purpose and considered calling a close to the Snowmass Conference. But talk of "the end" seemed to give a new energy to the dialogue that year, and they took up an old question: 'Should we not share something of what we have learned?' For by now there was an accumulated wisdom in the group. It was not that their answers were new, but that there were subtleties to them, real-world wisdom born of experience in the trenches of interreligious dialogue. It is always the simple things that are the hardest to understand and do.

In the end, they decided that they would publish a few memories and a series of aphorisms on what had made their dialogue work over the years in a commemorative pamphlet. Since I was acquainted with four of the ten members, it was suggested that I help them to shape just such a document. I agreed without much deliberation. But when I looked at their collection of "Points of Uniqueness," I immediately thought that their idea of a pamphlet was too humble; there was something here to be shared with a much wider audience in a small book.

So I interviewed all of the members to learn not *what* they had talked about, but *how* they had talked to each other. *What made this dialogue work? What were the bumps in the road? And how did they deal with them?* As much as people may have wanted to hear the details of what was undoubtedly a wonderful discussion of religion (me included), this was not what people needed to hear (nor was it in the spirit of the group's original intention).

Thus, *The Common Heart: An Experience of Interreligious Dialogue* is primarily a book *about* dialogue. It includes the Snowmass Conference "Points of Agreement," thoughts on "Spiritual Authority and Ethics," and some reconstructed dialogue. But as wonderful as these pieces are, they are merely the by-product of a profound relationship. The Snowmass Conference members learned to appreciate one another as individuals, and how different religions inform and enrich the experience of an individual; and this is what we can learn from them as we continue to explore the same territory.

Paradigms of Ecumenism
as a Spiritual Practice*

The Theory and Practice of Dialogue
with Father Thomas Keating
& Swami Atmarupananda

I FIRST MET Father Thomas Keating and Swami Atmarupananda in the Summer of 2002 in Aspen, Colorado. At the time, I was working on a small book about meditation in different religious traditions and attending an interreligious conference on the same subject, at which both men were teaching.[1] Immediately, I was struck by the profound erudition and deep commitment to spiritual practice exhibited by each man; these were living exemplars of Christianity and Hinduism, steeped in the wisdom and cultures of their respective religions, just as they were wrapped in the distinctive garb of their own monastic orders. However, as I began to talk with them, I discovered something still more interesting to me personally: as committed as each was to his own religious tradition (and concomitant practices), they were both

* This article was originally published in the *Journal of Ecumenical Studies* (Vol. 43, No. 1, 2008). The interviews it contains were conducted for the book, *The Common Heart: An Experience of Interreligious Dialogue;* the interview with Father Thomas Keating was conducted on June 1st, 2004, and the interview with Swami Atmarupananda on June 4th, 2004.

equally committed to ecumenism, and to dialogue *as a kind of spiritual practice.*

This led me to wonder—is dialogue an option, obligation or practice on par with say, reading the Vedas, *lectio divina,* telling a rosary, or saying *japa* over a *mala?* Moreover, is it legitimate to consider dialogue as such within a specific religious tradition like Christianity or Hinduism? Though neither man speaks directly to this question in these interviews, I would argue that it is.

Ecumenism exists on the margins of our religious traditions, like a bridge over a chasm connecting two continents. Because the bridge is open-ended, ecumenism in any one tradition will never be so distinctively Hindu or Christian as a Hindu *puja* or a Catholic Mass; nevertheless, on an arch over either side of this 'bridge,' Hindus and Christians will both inscribe their own mantras—"Truth is one, the sages speak of it by many names" (Rig Veda I, 164:46) and "In my Father's house are many rooms" (John 14:2).

This is to legitimize the activity from both sides, to say, 'This endeavor is fully in accord with my tradition. *In my Father's house are many rooms,* and I may visit them in order that I may truly know the fullness and splendor *of my Father's house.'* Thus it is clear that ecumenism is not so much to be identified with the 'rooms' as 'doors' between these rooms.

But if ecumenism is not an activity with any characteristics distinct to one religion or another, what then is its value to a particular religious tradition? On a basic level, ecumenism can be seen as a salutary attempt at getting to know one another better, to achieve a measure of understanding and tolerance; it is a means by which one may come to view one's own tradition and spiritual practices from another perspective, to discern the similarities and differences by dialogue and close observation.

However, on a deeper level (what Father Matthew Fox calls "deep ecumenism"[2]), it is actually an opportunity to learn about *oneself* while in full engagement with another, opening oneself to change—for in any true listening, there is always the possibility of being changed by the encounter. One might even choose to participate in the practices of another religious tradition, to engage in experiential learning or *"participatory epistemology,"* as Rabbi Zalman Schachter-Shalomi, one of ecumenism's pioneers, likes to say.[3] Such 'knowledge,' he suggests, can open one to an understanding of the deep structures, the basic technology beneath the Christian or Hindu exterior, discerning what is 'essential' from what may be considered 'accidental' (in the philosophical sense) in our own religious traditions. In many ways, this is what Max Müller had in mind when he paraphrased Goethe, saying, "He who knows only one religion, knows none."[4]

From this perspective, ecumenism and dialogue might be seen as a kind of 'diagnostic' to be run on our spiritual lives as well as our religious traditions—to see how well each is functioning—to be used as a tool for refining our own understanding of scripture and spiritual experience. And in this way, ecumenism might also be seen as a valid spiritual practice for every religious tradition in existence today.

The Snowmass Conference
& The Obstacles of Dialogue

In the years that followed my first meeting with Father Thomas Keating and Swami Atmarupananda, I found that as I was getting to know them better, they were already well acquainted. Swami Atmarupananda, it turned out, was a Hindu representative to the Snowmass Interreligious Conference, a well-known dialogue group convened by Father Keating in 1984. The Snowmass Conference (as it is generally known) is likely one of the world's longest continuously running ecumenical dialogue groups of its kind, if, indeed, there is another of its kind.

First convened as a private retreat for invited representatives of different religions, the conference has continued with only minor interruptions until this day. Recently, however, the Snowmass Conference has begun to rethink its mission. As the members have reached a certain maturity in their own dialogue with one another, they have begun to think that it might be time to take on the role of 'spiritual elders,' reaching out to those who would like to begin similar groups, to offer the benefit of their experience on a mentoring and apprenticeship basis.

In 2004, this general reorientation moved them to approach me to ask my help in collecting their experiential wisdom about the process of dialogue into a book. The result was *The Common Heart: An Experience of Interreligious Dialogue.*[4]

The interviews with Father Keating and Swami Atmarupananda that follow were simply two among many fascinating interviews conducted in preparation for the writing of *The Common Heart;* nevertheless, these two always stood out to me as exceptional for their clarity, contemplative depth, and penetrating insight.

In presenting these two interviews together, I wish to highlight three aspects of each that I feel are made stronger in juxtaposition. The first, as I have already pointed out, is a common understanding of ecumenical dialogue as a spiritual practice. The second stems from the interviewees' varied experience of and deep insight into actual dialogical situations. The third aspect follows up on the first: even if ecumenism is acknowledged as a valid activity within a tradition, the *manner* in which it is acknowledged is also important to dialogue—anything from mere tolerance of other traditions to a deep and abiding recognition of their essential unity with one another. Thus, part of my interviews with both Father Keating and Swami Atmarupananda follow this line of thought; however close they may be on the issue of ecumenism itself in these interviews, they clearly had very different starting points.

It is obvious to say that Father Keating, a Roman Catholic Christian monastic and former abbot, has very different commitments than does Swami Atmarupananda. Nevertheless, it is also necessary to understand the very different paradigms in which each man began his own ecumenical engagement.

For Father Keating, though beginning this activity in the new freedom afforded by Vatican II, there were still political and doctrinal issues to contend with, as well as difficulties in his own monastic community around this work. So, to my mind, Father Keating was something of a 'trailblazer,' having to find a path where none existed previously.

For Swami Atmarupananda, the situation was quite different. While he also had to work within the formal structure of the Ramakrishna Order, it is not quite an organization in the same sense as the Roman Catholic Church, nor has it ever had to 'accommodate' ecumenism as the Church has.

Inspired by Sri Ramakrishna Paramahamsa (1836-1886), a Bengali Hindu mystic, the Ramakrishna Order made Ramakrishna's insight that "all religions are true" and "all religions are paths to the One Reality" a central tenet of the order. Because of this, Swami Atmarupananda was able to make quite a different start on the ecumenical path.

Nevertheless, as we will see, this freedom brought with it other obstacles, perhaps more subtle, but equally difficult to navigate. So while both men share substantially the same view of ecumenism at the time of this interview, we may learn different things from their respective journeys: from one, we may learn something of the history of dialogue in the West, and from the other (a Westerner who went to the East), we may learn about the issues practitioners of all religions will face in the future as ecumenism achieves greater and greater legitimacy and acceptance.

Trailblazing Ecumenism:
An Interview with Father Thomas Keating

Netanel Miles-Yépez: How did a good Roman Catholic and Cistercian monk like yourself come to be involved in interreligious dialogue? There can't have been much of this happening when you made your first ecumenical forays into that territory.

Father Thomas Keating: Well, it's true; when I started, there weren't many Roman Catholics involved in interreligious dialogue. Thomas Merton was really pushing the boundaries writing about Zen in those early years before his death in 1968. He was definitely a pioneer in this area, and I had been privileged to see some of his unpublished conferences from that time.

Nevertheless, it was the documents of the Second Vatican Council that eventually opened up this possibility for me in a real way. At that time, most of the Christian traditions wouldn't touch the Eastern religions with a ten-foot pole! So there wasn't much incentive to study that material. It was looked upon with a certain hesitation, because it was thought that it might injure the Christian faith. Everybody had a different perspective, but often those perspectives were caricatured and misrepresented by ignorance and anxiety about the purity of doctrine.

The Second Vatican Council made a 180-degree turn in its attitude, and one particular document of the council spoke specifically about ecumenism with both Christian denominations *and* non-Christian religions. Those documents were liberating in that they gave people the freedom to pursue this possibility openly. I certainly experienced freedom, and I might never have done so otherwise.

N.M-Y.: Why is that?

T.K.: You see, I felt a great loyalty to the Christian scheme of things and never wanted to dilute the faith in any way for those whom I was trying to encourage in the contemplative lifestyle, in pursuing the spiritual implications of the creed and the major doctrines of the Christian religion. So it was really an enormous change and step forward, and very few people were prepared for it.

N.M-Y.: What was the official vehicle of that dialogue within the Church?

T.K.: After the Second Vatican Council, a group called the North American Board of East-West Dialogue was formed. The initiative for this group came from one of the congregations at the Vatican, the Congregation for Interreligious Dialogue. Thinking that Benedictine monks and nuns were the logical people to engage in a dialogue with the monks of other traditions—given that both were interested in spirituality and a lifestyle that supported it—Cardinal Pignedoli approached the Abbot General of the Benedictine Order about this possibility. And because we Cistercians were of the same family, so to speak, we were also invited to take part in this East-West dialogue.

That first meeting was held at Petersham, Massachusetts, in 1979, and a board of trustees was put together. It took a while for the group to be well accepted in the larger Benedictine community, but we had, even at that first meeting, quite a spectrum of people who showed interest in it, including some Cistercian abbots, one of whom was me. Other participants were Robert Mueller of the United Nations, Juliet Hollister, Swami

Satchidananda, Fr. Basil Pennington, Brother David Steindl-Rast, and Raimundo Panikkar.

N.M-Y.: Were you familiar with the work of Father Panikkar at that time?

T.K.: I had read some of his books, and I have met him several times over the years. He gave a second conference on monasticism sponsored by the North American Board of East-West Dialogue, perhaps at Mt. Holyoke, from which came his book, *Blessed Simplicity*.[6] Unfortunately, I wasn't able to attend because I was in a prolonged sabbatical retreat on the mountainside at Snowmass for about five months. I would have liked to have been present there, but I didn't want to break up the retreat.

N.M-Y.: Was the meeting at Petersham when you first became involved in this kind of dialogue?

T.K.: No, I started getting interested in interreligious dialogue in the late sixties. I was abbot of St. Joseph's Abbey in Spencer, Massachusetts, from 1961 to 1981, and, a little before 1970, we began to invite speakers from other religious traditions to the monastery.

At the time, a number of Eastern religious teachers were coming to the West. Just a half hour up the road from the monastery was an Insight Meditation center that drew a number of outstanding *vipassana* teachers from the Buddhist Theravada tradition, and they often came down and visited us. One of these was Ajahn Chah. I was very impressed with him, and we had a great time together; he had the same kinds of problems in his monastery as I was having in mine, and we had great fun comparing notes. He was like an old shoe. He reminded me a lot of Pope John XXIII, whom I had met briefly, and whom I also admired greatly. He was really laid-back. He had a very strict monastery and I don't know what he was like there, but he was friendliness itself when he visited us. That was one introduction.

Another was Joshu Sasaki Roshi of Mount Baldy in Los Angeles. Just before we met, he was actually about to head for Europe to look for Trappist monasteries there, since he had heard ours were most similar to the Zen Buddhist monasteries of Japan. When he heard about St. Joseph's Abbey, he decided that he didn't have to go quite so far. He came and offered to give us a *sesshin*, and we accepted. After that, he came to the monastery about twice a year for about ten years offering *sesshin*. Fortunately, I was able to get to most of them and hear his teachings first hand. I was very impressed with him as well.

N.M-Y.: What was it about Sasaki Roshi that so impressed you?

T.K.: Sasaki Roshi's broad-mindedness was an inspiration to me, because he was looking to teach Christians Zen. For him, Zen was not the property of Japan or even Buddhism, but a kind of universal religious attitude. I admired that perspective and have adopted it in my own life. I found the little exposure I had to Zen extremely helpful, and Sasaki Roshi's *taishos* very mind expanding. He was of the Rinzai school and made a special effort to find Christian kinds of *koans* for us.

Recently, a Jesuit priest, Father Kennedy, received the *dharma* lineage of Bernie Glassman Roshi, the *dharma* heir of Maezumi Roshi. The *dharma* was formally imparted to him, and now he is a Christian who is entitled to teach Zen.

N.M-Y.: I like to call this 'dual-citizenship.'

T.K.: Well, I guess you could call it that!

N.M-Y.: The dialogue has obviously come a long way in the intervening years; were all the monks as inclined to dialogue as you were in the early days?

T.K.: No, this was brand new territory and not looked upon with great confidence by some members of the community that I was leading. In other words, you had to move with a certain discretion in these areas. When Sasaki Roshi put on the Cistercian habit and joined us in the refectory, it was a little shocking to some people, and they clearly wondered where the monastery was heading!

N.M-Y.: Were there any visits from representatives of traditions other than Buddhism? What about Hindus?

T.K.: Well, we had much less exposure to the Hindu folks. But we were pleased to host Swami Satchidananda and several teachers from the Transcendental Meditation movement.

In those days, most of my exposure to Hinduism was coming through my reading, and even that was fairly limited because of my duties as abbot. I had read some of the books that were popular at the time, like Christopher Isherwood's *Vedanta for the Western World*,[7] and we were very interested in the Hindu-Christian dialogue going on in India with Bede Griffiths, who visited us a couple of times. We also read the books of Swami Abhishiktananda with great interest. These Christians who were trying to live a monastic life in a Hindu culture made a strong impression on us.

N.M-Y.: A moment ago, you suggested that these visits were the cause of some tension in the monastery; did this limit the amount of dialogue you were able to do?

T.K.: When I was abbot, as much as I felt we benefited from these encounters, not all of the monks were interested. And with all the work that office involved, I couldn't really attend interreligious dialogues as much as say, Brother David Steindl-Rast, who was one of the pioneers in the New York area, especially in his dialogues with Eido Roshi. I really didn't have time to devote to interreligious dialogues until I resigned as abbot of St. Joseph's in 1981. But then came the Centering Prayer work, and though I didn't intend to, I started spending a lot of time responding to those requests.

N.M-Y.: Did Centering Prayer get started in 1981?

T.K.: Actually, the Centering Prayer work began around 1976 at St. Joseph's Abbey, after a year's trial of a method by Father William Meninger, basing himself on indications from *The Cloud of Unknowing*; but I wasn't expecting to continue with that work after I resigned as abbot in 1981. I was hoping to focus on dialogue.

Nevertheless, I became more and more involved with the Centering Prayer Movement over time, and this eventually grew into Contemplative Outreach at the end of 1984. There has been something of a tension for me in trying to serve both categories, both ecumenism and Contemplative Outreach.

N.M-Y.: Really? When I have observed you in interreligious dialogue or teaching Centering Prayer, you seem to move seamlessly from one category to the other, almost as if there was an intrinsic relationship between the two.

T.K.: Yes, there was a lot of interaction between the two, and it has grown over the years. It was all evolving at that time. You see, a great many Christians had joined one or another of the Eastern disciplines over the years because they couldn't find any spirituality in the Christian *milieu*, whether in churches, parishes, or schools; in fact, many have said to me that had they known there was a Christian contemplative practice, they wouldn't have gone to the East. Still, I think they have benefited by it, and although many have remained there, others have returned to the religion of their childhood because they really felt more at home there. And, with a practice that was comparable to what they had learned in Buddhism or Sikhism, they were able to continue their journey in continuity with the religion of their youth.

But that was not our reason for doing this work. The point was really just to renew the Christian contemplative tradition and to make it an option in the marketplace for those who would never have the opportunity or go through the difficulty of learning the comprehensive and integrated wisdom of those teachings.

N.M-Y.: Why did you feel this was a need?

T.K.: During my early encounters with teachers of other traditions at St. Joseph's Abbey, I met a lot of Buddhist and Hindu teachers and their students, and it was evident to me that they were benefiting from their respective practices. For example, there was a psycho-spiritual wisdom presented in the form of 'methods' articulated in Buddhist meditative disciplines that wasn't articulated in quite the same detailed and practical way in the Christian scheme of things.

Certainly these existed in the Christian tradition, but they were fairly diffuse and not quite so focused-in on a practical daily method with comparable psychological insights. It was as if these teachers and their students had arrived at the monastery saying, 'Well, here's our method, what's yours?' There was no answer; we really didn't have a method as clearly articulated as theirs.

For us, the monastic lifestyle was a structure, an environment conducive to spirituality, but it wasn't a method in the same sense. It certainly had many practical rules and disciplines, many of which are duplicated in almost all monastic traditions, but they didn't quite apply to the individual in the same way many of the Buddhist practices did. For instance, take *mantra* recitation from the Hindu and Buddhist traditions; this was present in the Christian tradition, but was not as well worked-out or directly applied to the individual—based on the individual's needs, temperament, and personality—as seemed to be the case in Eastern spiritual traditions.

N.M-Y.: It seems to me, looking back over your career and your writings, that you have spent a great deal of time and energy not only articulating a clear method, but also in making the psychological and contemplative sophistication of Christianity explicit.

T.K.: That's true. It was there, but it was distributed over a great number of books. In this work, I benefited a great deal from contemporary science and psychology, especially from developmental psychology, which I feel is an essential kind of truth that all of the world's traditions need to take into account. Likewise, I believe that the teaching about the Unconscious from Freud on has had tremendous consequences for the spiritual journey.

N.M-Y.: Do you see this development in your work as an outgrowth of those early dialogues with Buddhists?

T.K.: Yes and no. Keep in mind, I was teaching the contemplative dimension of the Gospel from the time I became Novice Master in 1954, and some of my books, like *Crisis of Faith, Crisis of Love,*[8] are conferences that I gave to novices in the early 1950s, which I later modified and presented to the community when I became abbot in 1961.

N.M-Y.: I feel there is a subtle move that happened historically that will probably be overlooked in the history of interreligious dialogue because the bridge is so short. When Zen and Tibetan Buddhism arrived on the American scene, it was their meditation that was drawing people initially. It seems to me that there was also a ferment and parallel interest in reviving the contemplative aspects of the Abrahamic traditions in the mid-to-late 1950s; it was happening at the same time with you, Rabbi Zalman Schachter-Shalomi, and Father Thomas Merton. This interest and activity very narrowly preceded the interest in interreligious dialogue. Perhaps there is a relationship between the two, an attempt to talk about the 'tools of the trade'? Is it possible that the growth that was happening in that sphere fueled and followed into what became a dialogical movement?

T.K.: Yes, there is no doubt that there was a movement of the Holy Spirit to revive those things at the same time, and that was partially due to the accessibility and interpenetration of different cultures.

One of Sasaki Roshi's students, Leonard Cohen, was the first person to tell me about the Hasidic mystical tradition of Judaism that was present in Poland, and which was virtually destroyed in the Holocaust. He told me that he would have been a part of that tradition if it was still accessible; instead, he hooked up with Sasaki Roshi.

Later, I met Rabbi Dovid Din, Rabbi Zalman Schachter-Shalomi, and his successor at Naropa University, Rabbi Miles Krassen, all of whom were continuing this mystical tradition and making its contemplative depths available to people.

N.M-Y.: After you resigned as abbot in 1981, what direction did you take?

T.K.: Jacob Needleman had visited St. Joseph's at one time (I think the first chapter in his book, *Lost Christianity,*[9] describes his visit there) and later invited me to give a talk in San Francisco to his group. While I was there, I also gave a talk to a Gurdjieff group, and that Summer I went to the Naropa Institute to take part in the Christian-Buddhist dialogues initiated by Chögyam Trungpa Rinpoche.

Later, in the Fall, I went to the Omega Institute in Rhinebeck, New York, where there was an interreligious group that included a number of outstanding people: Rabbi Dovid Din, a fabulous interpreter of the Hebrew Bible with whom I became close friends, and the Korean Zen master Soen Sa Nim, who started a big place in Providence, Rhode Island. He was delightful. He invited me to make a tour of South Korea with him, but I wasn't free to do that at the time.

N.M-Y.: You founded the Snowmass Interreligious Conference around that time, didn't you?

T.K.: I always saw myself as more of a 'convener' than a 'founder.' It was really just a big experiment in the beginning, and I didn't know how it would all work out.

I began planning it in 1983 after taking part in a series of Christian-Buddhist dialogues at the Naropa Institute in Boulder, Colorado. During these dialogues, I noticed that we, the dialoguers, weren't speaking to each other as much as we were addressing the audience. But, on the two occasions when the conveners succeeded in bringing us together a day before the conference, we got on very well and actually got to talk to one another as peers, albeit all too briefly. I asked myself what would happen if the whole point was just to get together and talk, without an audience? What if it was broader than just a Buddhist-Christian dialogue? So that was the initial motive for getting that first group of teachers together at St. Benedict's Monastery in Snowmass, Colorado, where this began, and where it got its name, the 'Snowmass Conference' (though we didn't always meet there).

N.M-Y.: Was the primary purpose to take the dialogue out of the public arena, because you had noticed that the audience was influencing and impeding the intimacy of the dialogue?

T.K.: It seemed to me that it was *dominating* the dialogue. The rich interchanges glimpsed in those brief periods we spent together before the conferences began were all but non-existent when we came before an audience. I thought, let's just come together to talk about what helps us most in our spiritual practice. This, it seemed, would be far more fruitful, and hopefully we would come to a better understanding of the terms we were using to communicate. You know, you can use the same term; but if you are interpreting it in your own way, from your own cultural background, and the person you are dialoguing with is presupposing his or her own interpretation, then there is a lot of confusion.

N.M-Y.: How does a person's spiritual quality affect the dynamic of dialogue? After all, this must be a consideration in maintaining such a group?

T.K.: Well, I am certainly not qualified to judge anybody; but it is usually obvious that some people have been more exposed to the levels of spirituality that are considered more advanced in all the traditions, and it *can* affect the quality of the dialogue. Still, it is important to reserve judgment, remembering that everybody's contribution is nothing more than that, a contribution. We cannot discount that growth may also occur as a result of the dialogue itself.

N.M-Y.: Looking back, can you discern any development in yourself from the time when you began to dialogue, any assumptions that may have changed over time?

T.K.: Oh, sure! I certainly have a greater respect for and understanding of the other world religions; a greater openness toward and admiration for their methods and teachings; a greater sense of communion with the people who are practicing; and a sense of the oneness of human nature. It has greatly expanded my own worldview and understanding of the Christian religion and, if anything, has deepened and enriched it. I find a lot of insight in dialogue that helps me to better understand the Christian scriptures, or to explain them from a more contemplative perspective. In every way, I feel that it is enriching and valuable.

N.M-Y.: What effort was necessary to bring that about?

T.K.: In the beginning, given the narrowness of my perspective, it required a strict discipline of trying to bracket my own ideas and to be open to seeing them from a different perspective. True dialogue is an ascetical discipline; it really is quite searching at times and challenging to one's own presuppositions. Sometimes you are left trying to figure out how it all fits together: How can I explain this from a Christian perspective? How do I recognize and uphold the truth of this non-Christian presentation in the Christian worldview? Sometimes the two seem opposed, and it requires some soul-searching reflection and a willingness to change.

Ultimately, I find it liberates one from aspects of one's tradition that are cultural and not of the essence of the teaching. Usually, these have become so intermingled with the essence over the centuries that you cannot discern the difference without being challenged to look at the whole thing from an objective perspective—and that isn't so easy to do. It requires time, energy, and courage, but I have felt impelled to do that in my dialoguing, especially as part of the Snowmass Conference.

N.M-Y.: So real dialogue requires a certain spiritual *askesis,* or 'training'?

T.K.: That's right. Often the question is: How in the world am I going to harmonize this with what I have always taught and believed? The answer is: You have to go slowly and be willing to unwrap your pre-packaged values. It's a demanding discipline.

Those who don't have a good grasp of their own traditions (and I am afraid that is the majority of religious people) should go into dialogue advisedly. Often, when these people get into the deeper aspects of dialogue, they don't quite know how to handle it. You need to have a point of departure for discussion and evaluation and some sense of what is non-essential in one's own belief system.

It is a process of unfolding over a long period of time, an openness to the subtle changes that take place in oneself, an open vulnerability to the wisdom of other teachings. Now I find this very enriching and enjoy it. Hearing the explanations today, they no longer seem contradictory to anything in the Christian mystical tradition. It wasn't always that way, so that is some sort of progress, though perhaps others will think it a regression.

N.M-Y.: What was the basis of dialogue in the Snowmass Conference?

T.K.: Well, if our proximate goal was friendship, the ultimate goal was to really understand the religions of the world from the inside, from the perspective of someone who had practiced and benefited from them. For several years—maybe the first four years of the Snowmass Conference—we tried to see if we could come up with any agreements on the spiritual level.

We came up with a set of principles that we agreed on, and it was really quite surprising. It wasn't as though there was absolute agreement, but we felt comfortable enough to say 'yes' to them, though we might have preferred to express them a little differently here and there. Nevertheless, it does represent a commonality that is very significant and very striking. We called these our "Points of Agreement." I have been asked to publish these in several places. They were even in the "Report" of the World Parliament of Religions that happened in Chicago after the hundred-year hiatus.[10]

After that, we moved on to sharing common elements in the way of practice, like fasting, spiritual reading, guidance, chanting, trying to lead daily life from a meditative motive, from the contemplative space—all of those things that are common. All of the religions have practices like these, though some emphasize one more than another.

N.M-Y.: Did you do any work on the Points of Agreement in preparation for the first Snowmass Conference in 1984 or did they come solely from the dialogue?

T.K.: I think there might have been a draft of a few points that we used as a point of departure. Some we threw out right away, and others we continued to work on. We revised it again the next year and for about four years total; then we started discussing our differences. And that was very interesting, too, but we didn't feel it was necessary to make a list of them!

N.M-Y.: Speaking of differences, have you found any way of working with a fundamentalist position in dialogue?

T.K.: [Chuckles] Not so far! They are not very willing to speak to me; they think I am a disaster. They have a very literal interpretation of scripture which can be very frustrating and painful because it doesn't do justice to the text or its transformative potential. There is a meaning behind the text and a mystery to which it can only point.

N.M-Y.: What do you feel is the primary purpose and contribution of dialogue today?

T.K.: There is a mutual enrichment and sharing in deep dialogue that gradually dissolves suspicion and allows the religions to work together in the world. On the other hand, I also think that basic understanding, friendship, and respect are contributions we can make to the invisible spiritual world of humanity through our dialogue, and I believe that right disposition affects everybody, whether they can see it or not.

Universalism and Ecumenism: An Interview with Swami Atmarupananda

Netanel Miles-Yépez: Swamiji, in the Ramakrishna Order, there is an open door to interreligious dialogue through Ramakrishna Paramahamsa because of his own personal engagement with other spiritual traditions. Would you tell us something about his 'dialogue' and how it affects members of the order to have his example?

Swami Atmarupananda: Most people involved in religion come into a particular tradition and follow that path through a lifetime. For most of us it takes a lifetime of dedication to make any significant progress on the path, while others may go the length of the path and come to a state of illumination, staying in that light until the body finishes its participation in this life. Now, illumination is conceived of differently in different traditions, but there is usually a relatively straight trajectory through a path to its culmination point. This is how Ramakrishna started out.

He was born into the Brahmin caste in India and he followed a particular path within Hinduism throughout his youth; but, after having a life-altering vision of the Divine Mother, he attained illumination and became curious as to how illumination happened in other paths. So he began to follow different trajectories within Hinduism, in each case attaining to illumination. He did this over and over in Hinduism and then turned to paths in other religions.

It should be stressed that Ramakrishna wasn't a synthesizer—using bits of different traditions and putting them together. His way was to follow a particular path in its detailed integrity until he came to the illumination of that path. For instance, when he followed Islam, he took a Sufi *pir* as a teacher, and lived as a Muslim, performing *salat* five times a day, until he had attained to illumination. Though he never had a Christian teacher, he read the Christian scriptures daily with a devotee of his until he had an experience of Jesus and, through Jesus, an experience of God in the personal and impersonal aspects—what would be called the 'Godhead' in the Christian tradition. So, in his own life, he tested different traditions and came to the conclusion that all spiritual paths lead to the experience of God, or Reality. No matter what their differences are, they are experiencing the same Reality in different aspects or expressions.

This is a conclusion wholly consistent with the Hindu tradition; but as far as we know, it had never been proven before in direct experience the way Ramakrishna proved it. So this teaching is at the core of the Ramakrishna or Vedanta tradition—the belief that all spiritual paths lead to Reality, personal or impersonal. This affects the tradition and its adherents, opening one first to the value of other traditions, and then to the value of dialogue itself.

N.M-T.: In my reading of Ramakrishna, there is an essential humility about him that allows him to be so open.

S.A.: One of the charming aspects of Ramakrishna's life was that he was not one who practiced and attained illumination in isolation, that is, in an aloof, blissful state of forgetfulness of the world. He always came back to the world—albeit a world transformed in his awareness—which he considered sacred, then sought out people known for their deep spirituality. In the very hierarchical situation of India, it was unusual for a highly 'realized' person to seek others out; it was understood that others should seek him out. But, in Ramakrishna's case, he searched for men and women who had attained spiritual heights and shared their company, learning from them and also teaching them. This was part of his humility and realization.

It wasn't just spiritually illumined people either; he also sought out people who were 'great' in other fields of human activity. He felt that wherever there is an element of 'greatness,' in any field, there is an element of the Divine Mother's power, and he wanted to show respect to that power.

Nevertheless, this example doesn't mean that every devotee of Ramakrishna or monk of the order is actively involved in ecumenism or interreligious dialogue. It does mean that it is an integral, respected part of the tradition that everyone is aware of, and thus it is open to anyone who wants to participate in it.

N.M-T.: Was this ecumenical feature important in your own introduction to the order?

S.A.: For me, it was critical; it was what attracted me to the order.

I was brought up in a Protestant Christian home, going to church every Sunday. I was involved in all manner of church activities, including the choir and youth group. But one day when I was sixteen, I was standing outside of church waiting for the service to begin after Sunday school, and suddenly a whole flood of ideas came to me. I had never had any serious religious doubts before and had never thought in such a disciplined way as I did then. It wasn't intentional—these thoughts just washed over me:

> We Christians know that Christianity is the only true religion, and we Protestants know that Protestantism is the only true form of Christianity, and my particular denomination, while believing most of the Protestants are good, certainly knows it is the best of the Protestants. So how was it, out of the billions of people in the world, I was one of the lucky few born into the best denomination of the only true half of the only true religion? If the world was created by God, as we were taught, and God was benevolent, why did He appoint me to be so fortunate?
>
> Now, my Catholic friends also believe that Christianity is the only true religion, but regard Catholicism as the only true half of that tradition. So if I had been born in Saudi Arabia, perhaps I would have grown up thinking that Islam was the only true religion, and my sect of Islam the best form of that religion. And if China (these are the very places and traditions I thought of then) in a

Buddhist family, I would think that Buddhism is the only true religion, and my sect of Buddhism the best form of Buddhism. So it seems to depend on where you are born what you think is true religiously. They teach different things, so they can't all be true; they contradict each other in their exclusive claims, and so, it is most likely that none of them are true.

There on the spot I became an agnostic.

Shortly after that, I went to Sweden as an exchange student, which was fertile ground for an agnostic, as less than ten percent of Swedes at that time believed in God. I fed my agnosticism most of the year I was there until I came across an English book in a Swedish bookstore. It was called *Vedanta for the Western World*,[11] and on the back cover it said, "*Vedanta* respects all religious traditions. It believes that all religions are true, and that sectarianism (the claim to be exclusively true) is harmful. Religions are different because of the different cultures in which they arose, speaking different languages and having different rituals for different types of people, but all lead to the experience of spiritual Reality."

Here was a tradition that had looked at the same evidence I had, and, where I came to a negative conclusion, they had come to a positive conclusion! They are all true, it is just the exclusivist claim that is untrue; the language and forms that were the expression of it were different, but not the essence. I felt drawn to this positive conclusion, so I bought the book, took it home to the place I was living, and everything that I read in it seemed to ring true with something inside of me.

N.M-Y.: If I remember right, that is quite an ecumenical book. There is even a chapter on Brother Lawrence from the Christian tradition by Gerald Heard or Aldous Huxley.

S.A.: Actually, that was the other thing that sold me on the book; it had a number of essays by Aldous Huxley, whom I had already read and admired greatly. I thought that if he liked this tradition, then I am pretty sure I will too.

N.M-Y.: After you joined the Ramakrishna Order, did you continue to pursue your ecumenical interests, or did you find yourself needing to become more grounded in that tradition?

S.A.: When I first joined the order, though I loved the Vedanta philosophy, I had been studying Chinese Buddhism for a while, and, for the first several years I was in the order, I felt culturally more akin to things Chinese. I had even studied Chinese and kept my Chinese texts with me in the monastery. Everything Chinese I loved, and this became a real conflict for me for several years. As if that weren't enough, I also developed a great love for Catholic and Eastern Orthodox mysticism and monasticism. All of these traditions were pulling at me and I didn't know precisely where I belonged . . . "Vedanta is wonderful," I thought, "but, what if . . . ?"

After five years in the order, I went to India to stay for seven years. The first two years in India I spent in our training college at our headquarters. I studied Sanskrit and the scriptures and enjoyed it immensely; but still I kept my Chinese language books, which I had not been able to pursue for some time. I still had the idea that I would do so. When I did papers in the training college, if they were to be on religious thinkers other than persons in my lineage, instead of picking thinkers in the Hindu tradition, I would do Nagarjuna, the great Indian Buddhist philosopher, and Wang-Fo, the Chinese Zen teacher. So that interest was still very active, and the source of a mild conflict.

When I finished the training college, I was going by taxi to Calcutta, and suddenly there was a very clear moment when I realized that some of my deep psychological structures had shifted. It had been years in the making, but I suddenly saw it: my identity was now completely rooted in Vedanta; my spiritual identity had solidified in this tradition. It was a striking experience, and I can still remember it quite clearly. After that, I gave away my Chinese books; I no longer needed to keep that secret option open.

I continued to love and respect Buddhism and Christianity, but now it was from the standpoint of Vedanta; I no longer felt a conflict as to where I actually belonged.

Later, as an assistant editor for *Prabuddha Bharata*, 'Awakened India,' a Vedanta journal in English, I wrote a series of articles on Christian saints and the *bodhisattva* ideal of Buddhism from the standpoint of a Vedantist. So that was an important shift in my internal life.

N.M-Y.: Would you say that being rooted in the tradition, and knowing it, heightened and clarified your approach to ecumenism?

S.A.: Very much so. One of the riches we have today (that was never possible before) is access to all of the world's spiritual traditions. In any metropolitan area are teachers of almost every tradition you can think of, and even in small towns there are bookstores and libraries with books on these traditions. The downside is that, with so many choices, often one cannot settle on the one tradition most appropriate to oneself, choosing instead to remain an eternal seeker, never finding a tradition and deepening within it. It is possible to incorporate into one's spiritual life ideas from various traditions, but in my experience, this can only be done helpfully and healthily if we are rooted in a particular tradition and practice, taking wisdom from the borders and incorporating them into our center. But if we don't have a center—just little bits from here and there—we're not really going anywhere with anything, so we have to have depth, and a place to access profundity. That is our tradition and practice within that tradition.

After my experience of becoming rooted in Vedanta, I could understand the depths of other traditions, because I understood the depths of my own. I could then assimilate wisdom from elsewhere into my own practice. Before becoming rooted, there was internal conflict (and competition); it was like trying to go East, West, North, and South, all at the same time, and always feeling a little disoriented. Afterward, I knew I was going North, but could turn and take in the beauty of East, West, and South, and then continue on my journey North. In the end (and here is where the directional analogy fails), all of these paths end in the same place; but you have to walk one to get to that place of depth.

N.M-Y.: How did you become involved in actual dialogue?

S.A.: After I came back to the United States, five years after this experience in the taxi, I went to California and was there for fifteen years. Over time, various invitations came for me to speak to church groups and college classes about Vedanta and to compare it to other traditions. Eventually, I helped to found the Interreligious Council of San Diego. It was an active council and did important work, facing social problems with a united front, but it was not inwardly satisfying for me, because its purpose was not to share on an intimate spiritual level. It was important work; it just didn't have the dialogical dimension I longed for.

Nevertheless, it led to other opportunities. Because of my involvement in that group, I was invited to the Archdiocese of Los Angeles to have a Hindu-Christian dialogue on the topic, "When Religion is Not Enough: Discovering Your Own Spirituality."

Then, in the early 1990s, I was asked to become a member of the Snowmass Conference, a well-known ecumenical dialogue group started by Father Thomas Keating in 1984. I had long been familiar with this group and was thrilled when I was asked to join. At that time Gayatri Devi and her successor, Sudha Ma, were no longer able to come to meetings, so I was asked to represent the Hindu tradition in the group. Actually, the first year I was asked to attend as a guest, and afterward was asked to join as the Hindu representative.

More recently, I have been very involved in the interspiritual seminars of Edward Bastian's Spiritual Paths Foundation held around the country, which seem like an extension of the Snowmass Conference, as its founder, Ed

Bastian, is a member of the conference, as were a number of the speakers.

N.M-Y.: Part of the uniqueness of Father Keating's Snowmass Conference was his decision to take the dialogue out of the public arena and bring it into an intimate setting, where everyone could speak openly. How did it feel to finally engage in a dialogue where it didn't matter who was listening? Did it change the dynamic for you?

S.A.: It changed the dynamic in a very positive way. This was a dialogue where we didn't have to think about our 'public face,' but only about what was in our hearts; we could share openly with people who weren't going to go out and say things out of context and make difficult situations for any of us. This was one of the most attractive features of the Snowmass Conference.

N.M-Y.: Even when one doesn't have to maintain appearances, we still have our commitments, our 'rooted-ness' in a tradition, so what remains of the 'public face' that is important in the dialogue or that may hinder it?

S.A.: Obviously, there would not be much use in having a Hindu or a Muslim in a dialogue-group who couldn't really represent their tradition, that is to say, one who didn't have the essential knowledge of the tradition and rooted-ness in it—losing the 'public face' doesn't mean becoming an amorphous spiritual entity with no perspective and depth. The absence of the need to protect a 'public face' simply allows us to speak from the standpoint of our tradition, but more personally than a flat theological stand would allow.

I have had positive and negative experiences with the 'public face' in dialogue. Some people have a much harder time than others relaxing into the dialogue situation, and some are not able to overcome it. In that instance, the person is bound-up in an organizational, dogmatic identity that will not allow them to speak openly.

N.M-Y.: I remember Raimundo Panikkar, a Catholic priest with deep connections to the Hindu tradition, saying, "I can say whatever I like, as long as I make it clear that I am not speaking for the Catholic Church."[8] He has a certain freedom, but makes it clear what is his own personal view and what is the Church's doctrine. Is what the 'organization'—the Ramakrishna Order— thinks a consideration for you in public dialogue?

S.A.: The Ramakrishna Order is concerned with upholding the essence of the tradition and doesn't take many organizational positions that all members have to uphold. For me, it isn't a big issue; but for others, it is a major consideration. No one can tow a hundred percent of an organizational line; people are too complex to do that.

N.M-Y.: From your point of view, what are the strengths and weaknesses of the 'dialogue of theology' and 'defining the differences'?

S.A.: Too often, theology is born of a situation where an intellectual (not necessarily spiritually experienced) has read scripture and then considered the rational implications for the tradition. But, from a vedantic standpoint, at least ideally, theology is only an explanation for experience. When we just intellectualize, without understanding the inner experience, it can obscure rather than clarify. Certainly, in Hindu philosophy you will find plenty of fine distinctions that can get divorced from experience, but it is ideally understood that, to be a true theologian or philosopher, one has to be a person of deep experience; first comes experience, and only then the explanation in rational terms, the means by which it can be conveyed from one mind to another.

This is even more important in philosophy because it speaks more in terms of principles that any educated mind, whether Chinese, Indian, African, or American can understand. Theology, however, exists within a cultural and mythological context. Nevertheless, these rational explanations become problematic when we use them to defend ourselves from others, to keep from listening to another who is saying something which our theology doesn't recognize. It can be used as a means of expression or as a means of defense and aggression. But as an explanation for the context of our experience, it is useful. In dialogue it is good to stick to experience.

Now, the differences are also important. Ramakrishna, as I mentioned before, insisted on keeping Islamic food laws, wearing the clothes of a Muslim, and doing everything according to Islam when he was following that path; he didn't want to be a Hindu taking a mere 'taste' of Islam; he wanted to experience what it was to be a Muslim. So, differences are important.

Often Hindus are rightly criticized for too glibly saying, 'We're all one, and it is all the same.' But that's not what the tradition says; that is just what people say who take a superficial view of the matter. A particular path has its own integrity, but there are accretions accumulated over time in a tradition that may not be essential, while other parts are completely integral. Unless you understand that, you can't really understand the experience of another person.

N.M-Y.: What are some of the lessons you have learned about the dynamics of what makes dialogue work?

S.A.: Well, the first thing is well enough known to be cliché, but the problem with clichés is that we forget the point of them, remembering only the words. Nevertheless, for me, the ability to listen and hear what the other person is actually saying is essential. Now, this kind of listening doesn't come from mere politeness, and this is a mistake that is often made; true listening can only happen if you sincerely believe that the other person is really trying to say something important. This may sound obvious, but it is not obvious at all. People are usually so focused on what they have to say that they don't really listen, and then they don't understand and think the fault is with the person they weren't listening to.

So we must have the willingness and the ability to listen—two different things. Some people are willing, but don't know how. You must come with the conviction that other person has something to say that is valuable. You may not agree with it, but they wouldn't be speaking unless it was meaningful to them. So, it becomes your task to find out why it is meaningful to them, what are they trying to say, and in what context are they saying it. All of these things have to fit together, and this is extremely important to a successful dialogue.

Vivekananda teaches—anybody who has thought deeply about life, human experience, and the cosmos, has something to say that is important. One may not agree with them, but it is important to listen. For instance, in the 1950s, to listen to anything that came from Karl Marx would be difficult for an American because of the rampant hatred for Communism current then; and though, as a religious person, I am obviously not a Marxist, I believe Marx had something important to say. He had thought a great deal about the human condition, and, though I may disagree with his solutions, his analysis of human problems has a lot to say to us still.

Likewise, I am not a Freudian, but the truth is, Sigmund Freud looked deeply into the human mind and had important things to say. It is not enough to dismiss him, saying, 'He was all about sexual repression!' Freud wasn't a Freudian and Marx wasn't a Communist—they were just trying to figure things out, and because of that, they learned important lessons.

So, there may be ways of looking at religion that are not natural to me personally, but I should not close them out either, saying, 'That poor misguided person; thank God, I know better.' You may not agree with everyone, but for dialogue to be rich, you should have the conviction that others have unique perceptions of reality, and if I really listen, I am going to learn something.

Of course, we must be realistic also; in any gathering of people, someone comes more to talk than to listen, and that is destructive to dialogue.

N.M-Y.: The philosopher Ken Wilber has a criticism of what often happens in dialogue today, that it is often "flat." You have a circle, and many viewpoints are expressed, but that is all that happens—it is just talk and remains flat—it doesn't have a spiral-dynamic to it, it doesn't ascend. So if dialogue isn't just 'talk,' what has been the fruit of dialogue in your life?[13]

S.A.: That is a very important point, and I agree with Wilber's criticism. This is often what happens. Dialogue is reduced to a "flatland" of two-dimensional views put out for everyone to see, but no one is changed by any of it.

For me, there is a deep learning that takes place: the intellectual encounter with another tradition from books is replaced by a positive confrontation with reality, with another person who actually believes this—and believes it deeply. You can read a book about comparative religions, and see them two-dimensionally, and even have a two-dimensional dialogue, but encountering another person of spiritual depth affects one personally. When you hear someone speak with depth and conviction, the experience is transforming.

I have also seen people who have entered dialogue with relatively narrow theological frameworks, and who, in time, expand in extraordinary ways through this encounter.

But, even beyond this, when the dialogue is good, we share an experience of flowing with a higher intelligence, our individual understanding seems uplifted into a collective sharing with something higher. In a sense, this is the most important aspect of dialogue. It doesn't always happen, but when it does, there is nothing like it. When we are immersed in the wisdom of that collective sharing, a higher understanding descends on all of the individuals involved.

Courage, Interreligious Dialogue & Engaged Buddhism*

Interreligious Dialogue and Spiritual Activism with Tania Leontov

TANIA LEONTOV IS an *'engaged* Buddhist.' You may have heard the phrase often enough in the Buddhist community; but every once in while, you need to stop and ask yourself, "What does it really mean to be an 'engaged Buddhist'?"

For some, the word 'engaged' is simply short for 'socially engaged,' in the sense of being socially active. But while this is certainly consistent with much of the thrust of Engaged Buddhism today, it is nevertheless a limitation on the full meaning of the phrase as Thich Nhat Hanh originally conceived it. For if we see it only as social activism, it suggests that either the Buddhism or the social activism is a mere adjunct, something added to the other. But Thich Nhat Hanh's Fourteen Precepts of Engaged Buddhism make it abundantly clear that social activism is a natural by-product of a fully 'engaged' Buddhist practice, something different from

---

* This interview was first published in *Spectrum: A Journal of Renewal Spirituality* (Vol. 3; No. 2, 2007). The interview itself was conducted on June 4ᵗʰ, 2006, after the release of *The Common Heart: An Experience of Interreligious Dialogue* that same year.

'book-Buddhism,' or Buddhism in name only. Engaged Buddhism is a kind of dialogue with life, with ourselves, other people, with other views, other religions, and with the planet.

In 1983, Tania Leontov, Director of Restoring the Soul: Faith and Community Partnerships and The Buddhist Coalition for Bodhisattva Activity, first began to discern what it meant to be an engaged Buddhist while in conversation with a Christian monk staying in her home. The monk was Father Thomas Keating, who was then participating in the Buddhist-Christian dialogues at the Naropa Institute, and who was just beginning to become internationally known as one of the founders of the Centering Prayer movement. Over the next twenty years, as part of Father Thomas' famous Snowmass Interreligious Conference, Tania Leontov began to expand her vision of spirituality and what it meant to be 'engaged' in a spiritual path.

Netanel Miles-Yépez: How did you come to be interested in Buddhism?

Tania Leontov: I was born Jewish, but I was not 'religious' growing up. The closest I came to a spiritual experience was when I would find refuge in a neighborhood church, simply experiencing the peace of the place when things were hard at home.

Otherwise, religions weren't particularly interesting to me. By the time I was twelve, I had already come to the conclusion that there was no such thing as God. So, I guess, even then, I was on the path to Buddhism!

N.M-Y.: And how did you find your way to Trungpa Rinpoche?

T.L.: By an unusual route! I was in New York helping out with an *avant-garde* theater group, on a play called *America Hurrah*, which was one of the first major dramatic expressions in the anti-Viet Nam war movement. The playwright, Jean-Claude van Itallie, and the director, Joseph Chaiken, were friends of mine, and they had invited me to come to London where the play was being performed.

Of course I went. The play had a run in one theater, and was supposed to continue in another; but the British censor wouldn't let us reopen, because the script was really nasty about L.B.J. [President Lyndon B. Johnson]. So there we were with two weeks off, and our director suggested that we all go and visit a Vietnamese monk in northern London. He said it would be good to talk to someone who actually had something at stake, to authenticate what we were saying in the play.

So we journeyed to the Thai *vihara* where this monk was staying. While we were there, I came across a room full of people doing *metta* (loving-kindness) meditation . . . The feeling in the room was so lovely that I began to go there occasionally to meditate.

Not long afterwards, I saw a notice for a Buddhist "summer school," and I thought, "Well, it's something to do for a couple of weeks."

On the first night, I met an attractive British actor and he said, "Why don't you come to one of the classes given by my teacher? He is a Tibetan *lama.*"

It turned out that he had been reading *The Tibetan Book of the Great Liberation* and had decided that he needed to have a Tibetan teacher.[1] He looked 'Tibet' up in the phone book and found Tibet House. He called them up and said, "I want to study with a Tibetan teacher," and they said, "Well, we think there is a real one at Oxford." So he went up to Oxford and met Trungpa Rinpoche!

At the summer school, you could go to three different offerings simultaneously. I had no preferences, so I went to the talk given by Trungpa Rinpoche.

Now let me preface this by saying, I had done a lot of acid previously, but had stopped when I realized how important it was to me. To the other people in the theater group, it was *"just acid,"* but I felt that the experiences I was having had something to do with a profound aspect of reality that I couldn't quite express. Trungpa Rinpoche came out, and to me, it looked as if he was glowing golden. He started talking about some of the things I had experienced in my acid trips as if they were ordinary reality and I was blown away. I felt as if I were having an acid trip without anything to precipitate it except his presence! I was terrified. Afterwards, my friend took me to meet him. I shook his hand, and I said, "I'm sorry, you scare me very much . . . I'll talk to you later." I can't remember if I saw him at all during the rest of the summer school.

N.M-Y.: This must have been sometime between 1964, when Trungpa Rinpoche received a Spaulding Scholarship to study at Oxford University, and 1969, when he left for his solitary retreat in Bhutan?

T.L.: It was 1966, I believe.

N.M-Y.: When did you next encounter him?

T.L.: After I left summer school and was getting ready to go back to the States with the troupe of *America Hurrah*, I got a call from the actor, and he said, "Why don't you come up and visit me at Trungpa Rinpoche's meditation center [Samye Ling Meditation Center in Eskdalemuir, Scotland]." I liked him, so I thought, "Great!"

He picked me up at three or four in the morning at the train station at Langholm and said, "This is the only time you'll see me because I'm in retreat. So you're on your own."

I thought, "What! What am I doing here?" To tell the truth, I found the retreat facility disturbing. It was a dark hunting lodge with huge stone walls, and it was very cold inside. There were thirteen people there, including three Tibetans: Trungpa Rinpoche, Akong Rinpoche, and Sherab Palden Beru, the painter; a bunch of extremely uptight and solemn English people; and myself. I think there was another American, but he was crazy. He was very tall and walked around in a black *chuba* the whole time.

But as grim as the environment seemed, every once in awhile Trungpa Rinpoche would appear and I was completely enraptured with his teachings. I loved the meditation. I would go into this really hideous shrine room filled with an incongruous collection of Buddhist statues from Thailand, Japan, and Nepal, etc. They didn't look at all good together and produced long creepy shadows because of the candlelight. But I spent a lot of time meditating in there (wrapped in a blanket because there was no heat), thinking, "What is a little Jewish girl from Brooklyn doing in a place like this?" Nevertheless, it felt more like home than anything I had ever experienced.

When it came time to leave . . . I didn't. I told my friends in the theater group that they could take anything they wanted from my apartment in New York. I was staying here now. They felt betrayed, and I felt badly about it, but I stayed until the end of '69 when I finally came back to the States.

N.M-Y.: Was it in Scotland that you were first authorized to teach in the community by Trungpa Rinpoche?

T.L.: Yes—actually, I was authorized to teach before there was a real community! It was a pretty loose configuration of people in those days.

N.M-Y.: Who were you teaching then?

T.L.: In the beginning, it was a sort of 'auxiliary' teaching. Trungpa Rinpoche would be the primary teacher, and he'd call on me and tell me what he wanted me to talk about to a group. He had started a Glasgow group and an Edinburgh group, and I would teach there.

Later, when he first got here [America] to Karmê Chöling, he would go down to Boston to teach and I would also go in an auxiliary capacity. Later, he sent me to Burlington to talk about meditation. But after I got married and went into business, I stopped teaching for a long time.

N.M-Y.: How was it then that you came to be a representative of the Tibetan Buddhist tradition in the Snowmass Interreligious Conference?

T.L.: Well, in 1983, Father Tom was participating in the Buddhist-Christian dialogues at the Naropa Institute. These were important dialogues with excellent teachers representing Buddhism and Christianity. There was Brother David Steindl-Rast, Judith Simmer-Brown, Reggie Ray, Mother Tessa Bielecki, Father Tom, and of course, Trungpa Rinpoche. I only met Father Tom at that time because I was hosting him in my home on Mapleton Hill in Boulder. We had some very inspiring conversations of our own.

One evening, when he returned from the dialogues, he told me how there had been a little time in between the public dialogues where the participants actually got time to relax and talk together. He said, "I think if we could just come together informally, it would be a very rich dialogue." He said that he had been a part of a number of wonderful dialogues, but he regretted that there were always some participants who felt pressure to "represent," or to be "standard bearers" for their tradition's dogma and view when the dialogue was held as a public event. He proposed a private retreat for a group of interfaith leaders where they would get a chance to talk without having to support a "public face." He felt that this kind of intimate personal dialogue might be more productive in terms of true interfaith cooperation and appreciation. He also hoped that changes might come from this kind of deep sharing, bringing a measure of peace and sanity to the world, and said, "It is our responsibility to take part in these kinds of dialogues."

Well, when I heard this, I was possessed by a total passion to be a part of it! I couldn't say why, but I simply had to be part of it. Before this, I hadn't any interfaith interest, but in that moment, I knew I wanted to be there like nothing else.

My real question was, how? I didn't feel particularly qualified; I was a teacher of Buddhism and Buddhist meditation, but I was not remotely a spiritual leader in the sense that Father Tom was. Nevertheless, it was weighing on me. So after wrestling with my doubts, I finally called him and said, "I realize I am putting you on the spot . . . and trading on our friendship . . . but I want to be part of this retreat. I'll understand completely if you say, 'No.'" . . . But he didn't.

N.M-Y.: Do you know why you had to be a part of it now?

T.L.: Interfaith related work is almost all that I am doing now in terms of both my livelihood and my passion. I didn't know where the inspiration came from, but it continues to shape my life in a profound way. Father Keating was right: there is wisdom held in our spiritual paths that the world needs badly, a contact with something vast in our narrow lives, a small opening that might help to change the terrible things that are going on in our world.

N.M-Y.: Where did the inspiration for the Snowmass Conference go from there?

T.L.: First, Father Tom went about gathering the people. This wasn't difficult for him. He had many contacts and was able to draw major teachers without much trouble. There was Douglas Steere, the head of the Quaker Religious Society of Friends; Srimata Gayatri Devi a Vedanta lineage holder of the Ramakrisha Order, who was an old friend; Rabbi Rami Shapiro and Imam Bilal Hyde, whom he knew from Lama Foundation; Pema Chödrön; and Father Thomas Hopko, a Greek Orthodox priest. There was also Grandfather Gerald Red Elk, whose meeting with Trungpa Rinpoche is well-known; and Bernie Glassman Roshi, then *sensei*.

Glassman had already started the Greyston Mandala and was a good friend of St. Benedict's Monastery (where Father Tom lived). He helped them get into the cookie business when they were having trouble finding the proper balance between a good income stream and 'right livelihood.'

N.M-Y.: What would you say it was that characterized this group as a whole?

T.L.: Well, I think it was made up of people totally committed to their spiritual paths, and, in general, I think they were non-conformists, even a little rebellious. I mean, they stood solidly in their traditions, but they tended to have much more flexibility than you usually find.

N.M-Y.: You also seem to have had the benefit of having a number of persons of deep spiritual quality in the group. That had to help in its success?

T.L.: Yes, it made a big difference. To be around genuine wisdom holders is a very different experience. In many ways, they are very 'ordinary,' but their view and presence also emanates something special. It makes a difference in the environment.

It's hard to say what their special quality is . . . they are just more accommodating than other people, but can also have a very sharp clarity that cuts through the nonsense. I am thinking of Gayatri Devi's razor sharp mind, and Father Tom's rapier-like thrusts at dogmatists! So, it's not just kindness, but their compassion is palpable. They also have a way of finding the unifying principles and helping to expose them. When they speak, there is a sense of enormous courage. If you are on a path with them, just being in the presence of these qualities invites your own best qualities to emerge. It makes you understand what humans are capable of, and what you are capable of . . . When you quail and hide-out, and see someone genuinely, and with great simplicity, being very brave, you can feel it, and it helps to create a map for you of where you need to go. Those of us who have come across spiritual masters carry that map with us, the sound of that voice in our ears, and the feeling of their compassion in our hearts. It makes a tremendous difference. There was at least one year when Father Tom couldn't attend, and I felt that the light almost went out of the group. There was a sense that we were more likely to end up in 'smaller mind' without him!

N.M-Y.: You mentioned "courage" . . . It seems to me that courage is also a necessary part of dialogue.

T.L.: To really listen takes courage.

N.M-Y.: Yes, you have to say, 'I come with all of this *knowing,* but I have to be willing to let it all go . . . to be willing to be convinced of something else, if I am really listening.'

I have noticed in our conversations over the last couple of years that courage comes up a lot for you.

T.L.: Courage has always been very moving to me. People don't often realize their true strengths, or the extraordinary courage it takes just to be a human being— even in the most ordinary ways. I used to look at my parents and think of them as my "little parents," because I felt that they were timid, that their lives were built on fear; but now I think, "How courageous they were. They created a life, they bought a house, they had a child—it takes real courage to live an ordinary life. It takes courage just to cross the street!"

Life is wild, you know. When I used to look for a unifying factor in Trungpa Rinpoche's students (who were truly diverse), I found that they all seemed to be attracted by the smell of the wild. He was truly a man without boundaries, who lived in the moment, and you couldn't bring 'baggage' with you when you 'traveled' with him. You couldn't say, 'No, this is the way it is supposed to be.' You had to relate to things as they were in the moment. That to me was a stunning encounter, an encounter with that nature of mind that acknowledges the absolutely wild aspect of life.

I used to have a recurring dream where I was on a street filled with brownstones, and I didn't have a key to any of them! I had to come to terms with the fact that there was no safe and secure home; it's a wild life.

You see these geese flying overhead [points]—you know they fly, they look for food, for water, and then they roost wherever they are. In our culture, we have built barriers to protect ourselves from that intuition, that wild undercurrent. We make money, build houses, make more money, build bigger houses, make them more secure, inside and out, and that makes us feel better. But the safety is a fiction, because we inevitably die.

On the spiritual path, you are less and less able to ignore the fact that life is very wild. You can't write the script. Those are the kinds of things that make courage very interesting and attractive to me, and I see it all over the place. I don't think it is the purview of special people, but I don't think people often recognize the kind of courage that they have. You need it on a spiritual path because you have to surrender to something beyond yourself, if you want to make progress. When you think life is about 'driving the car' yourself, giving up that fictional power is very difficult.

N.M-Y.: What kind of courage was required of you in the Snowmass dialogues?

T.L.: Well, some of it was around giving up on my old assumptions. As I said before, though I was born Jewish, I was not a religious person growing up. So, even after I became a Buddhist, I had a very primitive notion of what Judaism and Christianity really were; I really had no idea what either was about.

When I was twelve, as I said, I came to the conclusion that there was no such thing as God, so, theism for me was always a marvel; I couldn't believe that anyone would allow themselves to be so "deluded." I questioned what it was in people that made them need that. It seemed to me that they were abdicating responsibility in a certain way.

I am sure I brought this to my earliest attempts at dialogue. But, as I began to have more exposure to the subtle understandings of God, through the lens of Buddhism, I felt that the difference was so subtle, that in most ways, it didn't matter that there was a difference. There certainly was a difference in how people spoke about things, but the mystical understandings seemed very close.

When I first met Father Keating and Srimata Gayatri Devi, it had never occurred to me that a Christian or Hindu could attain 'enlightenment.' I thought of enlightenment only in terms of Buddhism. But with Father Keating and Ma, I felt that I was looking at the nature of enlightenment as it unfolds in other paths. I mean Father Tom evolved over a period of time, but I always felt that he was a vast soul. To see his boundless compassion and wisdom turned me around.

N.M-Y.: Perhaps this is what Father Keating had in mind in the beginning when he talked to you about the contributions to peace that such dialogues could make?

T.L.: Yes, I think that's right. I have learned so much, and a number of my assumptions have been overturned by what I have learned. That has made for some measure of peace not only in myself, but also allowed for friendship with many people I may never have even had the opportunity to meet otherwise.

In a very basic way, I just feel more at home in the world; people don't feel strange just because they believe differently. I feel I can approach many traditions easily because I now have had an intimate experience of them.

N.M-Y.: Over the years, have you gotten a sense of what makes for a good dialogue? What are some of the lessons you have learned about what makes a good dialogue work?

T.L.: You have to establish a basis of friendship, or you do not even get to *genuine* dialogue. You have to be courageous (for the reasons we have mentioned), but also because sometimes, what you are going to say will not suit everyone there. Nevertheless, you have to remain true to your own experience and understanding and say it anyway; you have to be thoughtful and precise in explaining what it is about, but still say it with courage. You also have to be willing to say, 'I don't understand,' or 'This is a question for me. Can we talk about it further?' You are there as a contributor and you have to have the dignity and the courage of that role . . . to be both vulnerable and honest.

N.M-Y.: What has been the 'fruit' of this dialogue for you?

T.L.: Well, there have been a number of things that have come up in my life as direct and indirect results of my participation in the Snowmass Conference.

The first concerns my teaching. Over the years that she was involved in the Snowmass Conference, Gayatri Devi took me under her wing, and I felt mentored by her. As I said before, even though I was one of Trungpa Rinpoche's first teachers, after I got married, I stopped teaching for a long time. At one point, Gayatri Devi invited me, out of nowhere, to come and teach at her *ashram.* It was a terrifying experience. I literally shook on stage, but I was so grateful to her; and who knows why she did it.

Then, every once in a while, simultaneously with times when I was feeling down, there would come in the mail a box of *prasad* (food dedicated to the gods) from her shrine, or a little gift.

Once, she sent me one of her cashmere meditation shawls, and invited me to come back and teach. That was the maternal aspect of the *guru.* We didn't have many personal conversations, but her quality, her vastness, her compassion were beyond measure, and always present.

N.M-Y.: Are you still teaching?

T.L.: Yes, and the reintroduction to it came through Gayatri Devi and other members of the Snowmass Conference. I mostly teach in interfaith situations now. That is to say, I talk about Buddhism to non-Buddhists, or teach religion generally in non-Buddhist institutions. For instance, this year, I have two invitations to give talks on the East Coast, at Glastonbury Abbey and at the Vedanta Centre in Massachusetts. I'm also going to Chicago to teach about Buddhism at a Benedictine conference. I also teach Eastern Religions and Adult Spirituality at Regis University in Denver.

N.M-Y.: Those are direct results of your participation in the Snowmass Conference. What about the indirect results?

T.L.: I am now the director of two small non-profits: the Buddhist Coalition for Bodhisattva Activity (nurturing partnerships between Buddhist sanghas and human service agencies)—outreach work; the other is Restoring the Soul: Faith and Community Partnerships, which is interfaith outreach.

N.M-Y.: How did you come to be involved in these?

T.L.: When I was working at the Shambhala Center (which I did for thirteen years) as one of the directors of family affairs, contemplative arts, and outreach, I found (since I had been part of the community from the beginning) that we seemed to be going over the same ground again and again: How do we treat elders? Who gets discounts at programs? Where are the children housed? It was the same thing over and over again, and I thought, "This is a group neurosis"—one that is perhaps true of every young faith community, but I felt refreshment was needed.

I had heard about studies that were done, particularly in the Lutheran Church, where they found that those congregations that were outwardly focused thrived, while those that were inwardly focused diminished. That struck me as true, and I thought, "That is it! We need to reach out."

So I tried a number of outreach projects that were not very successful. I just couldn't get people interested. The only people who were interested were the people who were already doing it.

One day, a survey came across my desk from an exploratory taskforce started by Terry Benjamin, who is the Executive Director of the Emergency Family

Assistance Association in Boulder, called Restoring the Soul. He had been inspired by the faith initiative that had come out of Washington, saying, "the faith congregations are really great resources for community welfare that are largely untapped." So he decided to do a survey, got a small grant to do it, and he started this taskforce. He sent the survey out to different congregations, and when it came to the Shambhala Center, it was passed over to me. So I answered the survey, and they said, "Would you be interested in being on our taskforce?" Of course, I said, yes. I volunteered on the taskforce for two years as a representative of the Shambhala Center.

We gathered information and got a good response to the survey. We found over 250 faith communities in Boulder County at every range of activity, from the very active socially to those who said, "Don't bother us; we are looking at our belly buttons!" We started to think, "Hey, maybe there is something to do here." At which point, Bruce Swinehart, the consultant working with Terry said, "It's turning in an action direction; that's not my thing," so they asked me to be director.

We began to work on collaborations and education programs: "brown bag" discussions and conferences. For me, the inspiration came directly from the Snowmass Conference; it just developed in a different direction. Restoring the Soul is about education on issues, and encouraging faith communities to collaborate with human service agencies. I meet with different faith leaders and talk with them about opportunities for collaboration. It's a very hard go—sometimes they're not interested at all, and sometimes, if they are, they still can't imagine why there is another entity interested in what they're doing. So now

I am spending time pointing out how 'service' is a core component of a number of spiritual traditions, especially Buddhism, Judaism, and Christianity.

N.M-Y.: There is a strong case to be made there for many traditions.

T.L.: It's amazing to me to find out how close they are to each other on this ground—that according to each, service is essential to being human, and to individual well-being. Well-being is not the house, the dog and the car, the money and the gourmet food—well-being is helping other people. I think people, in general, just don't know it. I mean, I started looking again at the Four Immeasurables of Buddhism, and it's all about service to others; that is the ultimate of well-being in all of these paths. Now I am working with faith leaders to develop study guides on service in the various traditions.

We have a Christian 'guide,' and a Buddhist one. For the Buddhist one, I got permission to use someone's master's thesis from Naropa University on the Bodhisattva path as the backbone. And for the Christian one, I went a lot to the Evangelicals, because they talk a lot about service; they want to live it. I softened it a bit, so it would fit more Christian denominations. Father Thomas read it and said that it would do. For the Jewish one, I am working with a local rabbi.

As I was working with Restoring the Soul, I thought we need a Buddhist parallel to this whole activity, so that the thirty or so Buddhist communities of Boulder County can work together as a coalition in the same way, serving others in the extended community of Boulder County.

I feel that interfaith dialogue confirmed a passion in me for collaboration, and also for the crucial part spiritual life has to play in all human endeavors.

PART III
Hasidism
& Jewish Renewal

"The Fourth Hasidism" by Netanel Miles-Yépez, 2014.

Foundations of a
Fourth Turning of Hasidism*

HASIDISM IS A movement of the spirit that arises in us as a yearning for God and the sacred, and which expresses itself through acts of loving-kindness and service to the same. Hasidism is the willingness to make ourselves transparent to God's grace and will, to live in the authentic presence of God—*nokhah p'nai Ha'Shem*—as if facing God in every moment, allowing this awareness to change our behavior, to make sacred acts out of potentially profane and purely secular moments.

This movement of the spirit, at the core of the Hasidic tradition, is also a universal impulse, as is the attitude of active-receptivity to the divine which it fosters. Thus, what has been called 'Hasidism' over the centuries is only the story of the evolution and manifestation of that universal impulse and attitude among the Jewish people—for whom it has become a communal *ethos*, wedded to the primary revelation of Judaism, to the Jewish myth and *magisterium*—with unique characteristics and experiential outcomes.

---

* Originally published as a small booklet, *Foundations of a Fourth Turning of Hasidism: A Manifesto*, in 2014. Although published in the name of Netanel Miles-Yépez and Zalman Schachter-Shalomi, it was written exclusively by Miles-Yépez shortly before Schachter-Shalomi's passing as a gift to him; it was among the last things he read.

From this perspective, Hasidism is both the origin and fulfillment of Judaism's spiritual potential, arising and developing in different periods to meet the unique needs of a specific time and place. Through the millennia, Judaism has witnessed the emergence of numerous Hasidic movements, both large and small, some bearing the name, and others not. Among the former are four significant Hasidic movements which represent the Hasidic ideal as it existed in three different paradigms and historical periods: the classical period of Greco-Roman Palestine; the medieval period of Muslim Egypt and Christian Germany; and the pre-industrial period of Eastern Europe and Russia.

We call these movements, 'turnings,' literally, revolutions that demonstrate the adaptation of the Hasidic tradition to a particular time and place.[1] Judaism, as we have already suggested, has seen three such turnings of Hasidism (in four separate movements), each an appropriate expression of the highest and most integrated levels of spirituality available in that period, which is to say, informed by the spirit of the times and influenced by the chthonic element of the place.[2]

The First Turning of Hasidism

In the Mishnah, we are told about the Ḥasidim ha'Rishonim, the 'First Hasidism.' Although this is likely a general reference to the 'pious of times past,' the examples given of their actions are consistent with what we know of Hasidism in other periods.[3] Moreover, in the classical period of Greco-Roman Palestine, we find references to a Jewish sect known as the *asidaioi* or *essaioi* in Greek, which may be the first actual community to be called Ḥasidim, as these words are generally believed to be Hellenized versions of Hebrew and Aramaic originals (most likely, *ḥasidei* or *ḥasya*, both meaning, 'pious').[4] In the Book of Maccabees, they are called "stalwarts of Israel, devoted in the cause of the Law."[5] And in the writings of Philo of Alexandria, it is said that they are "above all, devoted to the service of God" and seek "a freedom which can never be enslaved."[6] It is generally accepted that these Ḥasidim (usually called Essenes, based on their Latin name, *esseni*)[7] are the authors of the Dead Sea Scrolls and the sect whose practices and beliefs are described therein.

The Second Turning of Hasidism

The Second Turning of Hasidism is best seen in two movements of the medieval period, emerging independently in separate geographic areas and cultural climates which clearly influenced the particular expression of Hasidism in those places. These were the Ḥasidei Ashkenaz in Christian Germany, and the Ḥasidei Sefarad in Muslim Egypt.[8] The Ḥasidei Ashkenaz were led by the famous Kalonymous family of kabbalists (most notably, Rabbi Yehudah He'Ḥasid, the author of the *Sefer Ḥasidim)* who practiced an almost monastic form of Hasidism. The Ḥasidei Ashkenaz planted seeds in Europe that would spring up in many smaller Hasidic movements in the centuries that followed. Similarly, the Ḥasidei Sefarad were led by the philosopher-mystics of the Maimuni family (most notably, Rabbi Avraham Maimuni of Fustat, the son of Maimonides, and the author of the

Kifayat al-Abidin) who forged a community of Hasidic contemplatives whose teachings and practices paralleled those of Muslim Sufis, whom they openly admired.

The Third Turning of Hasidism

The Third Turning of Hasidism flowered in the pre-industrial period of Eastern Europe and Russia under the leadership of Rabbi Yisrael ben Eliezer, called the Ba'al Shem Tov, and his successor, Rabbi Dov Baer, the Maggid of Mezritch, whose lives and teachings set the pattern of Hasidism for centuries to come, even into our own day. Integrating and building on the spiritual work of previous Hasidic movements like the Hasidei Ashkenaz, as well as generations of kabbalistic endeavor, Hasidism exploded with creativity in the 18th-century. Its approach was characterized by a new embrace of the material world as a divine manifestation, an acceptance and celebration of the potential of the common Jew, a joyous engagement with life, prayer and contemplation of extraordinary depth, as well as stories and teachings that turned conventional thinking upside down. Owing to its positive approach and popular appeal, the movement spread like wildfire over Eastern Europe and Russia, making it the most influential of the three Hasidic movements.

The Fourth Turning of Hasidism

With the emergence of a global consciousness in the 20th-century, perhaps best articulated in the work of the philosopher Pierre Teilhard de Chardin and symbolized by the first images of our planet as seen from outer space, the paradigm of every known religion began to shift irrevocably. Before the dawning of this global consciousness, every religious tradition followed a more or less independent trajectory, or could at least maintain the illusion of doing so. But once the 'shape and sharing of the planet' was known, all trajectories began to align, causing upheaval in every religious tradition and spiritual lineage. Thus, a global consciousness is both the primary catalyst for, and the defining characteristic of, the Fourth Turning of Hasidism.

The following are common elements shared by all the previous turnings of Hasidism in the view of the Fourth Turning.

Repentance

The beginning and end of a Hasid's spiritual path is *t'shuvah*, continually 'turning' one's awareness back to the divine source, remembering from whence we come and our common identity in the divine being. *T'shuvah* is also repentance, a reorientation to a radical humility that serves as the foundation for true righteousness in our world. No matter how righteous one appears or feels oneself to be, there is always room for repentance; for the paradox of true righteousness is the requirement of self-abasement, realizing one's utter inability to serve God perfectly and humbling oneself in response.[9]

Prophecy

Nevertheless, the primary goal of Hasidism is a direct connection to God, often characterized as *nevu'ah*, 'prophecy,' or *ru'ah ha'kodesh*, the 'spirit of holiness.' Hasidism believes that the prophetic consciousness is still available (though the Sages declared the prophetic period closed at the time of the closing of the canon).[10] If Hasidism, as we have said, is a genuine 'openness to the divine will,' then prophecy is the product of such openness (as seen in the root of the word, *navi*, 'open' or 'hollow').[11] This suggests both the method and the means that allow for prophecy, or as we might characterize it today, deep intuition.

Prayer

The primary means of cultivating one's 'openness to the divine will' is prayer, which is central to Hasidic life. In the Hasidism of the Ba'al Shem Tov, prayer is generally spoken of as *avodat Ha'Shem* or *davvenen*, 'divine service' or 'prayer in which one is deeply connected to God.'[12] In the Fourth Turning, we are also inclined to emphasize what we call 'davvenology,' the investigation of the inner process of prayer, including all aspects of worship and the Jewish liturgical life. Today, it is not enough to be able to connect in prayer; we must also understand the sacred technology which allows us to make the connection.

Practices

And yet, Hasidism has also embraced a variety of supererogatory methods or *hanhagot*, 'spiritual practices' that are not required in Judaism, but which are taken on by the Hasid to continue the process of making oneself transparent to God's grace and will, and to facilitate an awareness of living in the authentic presence of God. Such *hanhagot* were often given in the form of traditional and intuitive *eitzot* or 'prescriptions,' to remedy particular spiritual maladies and to promote particular spiritual effects.[13]

Guidance

Spiritual prescriptions and guidance in the ways of Hasidism are given by one's *rebbe*, a *neshamah k'lalit* or 'general soul' who is able to locate and connect with the souls of individual Ḥasidim because they are part of the same 'soul-cluster,' allowing for relationships of deep spiritual intimacy. The *rebbe* gives their guidance to the Ḥasid in the private encounter, *yeḥidut*, and in public gatherings, *farbrengen*.

In the past, the person serving others as *rebbe* was often indistinguishable from the *'rebbe*-function' they performed. But in the Fourth Turning, it is recognized that the *rebbe*, though 'called to service' and to function as a *neshamah k'lalit* through the cultivation of their own spiritual attunement, is nevertheless, not identical with that service and function. For the projection of such a static identity limits the rebbe's personal freedom, creates unrealistic and unhelpful expectations, and allows the Ḥasid to yield personal responsibility in a way that is not conducive to spiritual growth.

Because the ability to function as a *rebbe* is rare, requiring particular spiritual gifts and a significant cultivation of them, Hasidism also recognizes the need for the *mashpiyya*, the mentor or guide, as well as the *ḥaver*, the spiritual friend. The former is an individual who has achieved maturity on the spiritual path and is thus able to help others in negotiating many of its paths and pitfalls. Likewise, friends who share the same spiritual values, and with whom one can share the journey, are also critically important.[14]

Community

The communal context for spiritual growth in Hasidism is the *farbrengen*, literally 'time spent together.' The Hasidic gathering may take place on *Shabbat*, other *yom tovim*, or at any other time of the year. Likewise, it may be led by the *rebbe* or a *mashpiyya*, or simply be a gathering of *haverim*. It is a time for spiritual guidance, cultivating both joy and introspection, during which meditations and Hasidic *niggunim* (melodies) are used for tuning consciousness to the right frequency for receiving Torah, and where Hasidic *ma'asiot* and *meshalim*, stories and parables, open the heart and imagination to the possibilities of living a more virtuous reality.

Law

The norms of Hasidic life and behavior are oriented around a radical engagement with Jewish law, or *halakhah*. Contrary to some modern misconceptions, Hasidism is not anti-legal and has never been casual about *halakhah*. On the contrary, Hasidism stresses the most integral, elevated, and meaningful application of every aspect of Jewish law and tradition to Jewish life. This is also the view of the Fourth Turning, which seeks to engage and examine every law and tradition, taking the needs of the time, the place, and the people into consideration, looking at the original function of the law in its original context to see how it may be best applied today to achieve similar ends.

Providence

Finally, the view of Hasidism is providential. In each turning, Hasidism has embraced an idea of providence in keeping with its own experience of divinity, as well as an awareness of the 'miraculous order' in creation. The holy Ba'al Shem Tov spoke of *hashgahah pratit*, a 'specific personal providence,' in which all events are seen as happening with a specific or particular purpose, beyond appearances of 'good' or 'evil.'[15] This is in keeping with his pantheistic worldview, wherein there is nothing in existence but divinity; therefore, nothing happens that is not divine or divinely ordained (however we may judge it according to our limited vision). Our own understanding of 'organismic pantheism' is but an extension of this view, merely acknowledging the dynamic and sophisticated organizing principle of ecological systems within the whole of possibility, always serving the greater purpose.

In one form or another, these elements have been present in every turning of Hasidism. And yet, each turning always contributes something *new*—new interpretations, new teachings, new practices and new ideas. The following are some of the new ideas on which the Fourth Turning bases itself:

Renewal

More than ever before, Hasidism needs to maintain an awareness of its own evolution (of which the various turnings are evidence) in the context of the greater evolution of spiritual traditions on the planet. As consciousness evolves over time and the world changes, traditions must reclaim their primary teleological impulse in order to adapt to the needs of the evolving consciousness. This process of unfolding within and adapting without, we call 'renewal.'[16] Renewal itself is characterized by the struggle to marry the *magisterium* of a religious tradition—its inherited body of knowledge and wisdom—to a new reality map or paradigmatic understanding of the universe.

On a small scale, renewal is happening continuously; but it is also a process that we witness on a larger scale in certain epochs or axial moments in history, like ours, when religions and religious forms are breaking down and slowly re-organizing and re-forming over time.

An awareness of this process can help to keep our current religions and spiritual traditions healthy. For as we engage and become aware of the process of renewal, we must re-evaluate our traditional spiritual teachings and practices, considering their 'deep structures,' analyzing their function in different historical periods to better understand how they might apply, or be adapted for use in our own time.[17] This new understanding and adaptation allows us to utilize the maximum of our historical traditions, without at the same time turning a blind eye to the true needs of the present.

Deep Ecumenism

However, as we explore the deep structures of our own traditions, revealing the basic functionality beneath the specific wrappings, we cannot ignore their similarity to those of every other religious and spiritual tradition on the planet. Providence, as well as our own evolutionary perspective, demands that we acknowledge a similar sacred purpose at work in these deep structures, that we learn how others use them for the fulfillment of the greater purpose, and how others can aid us in understanding our own use of them.

While dialogue with other religious traditions undoubtedly took place in our past, it had no legitimizing basis or support in the tradition, and could rarely take place openly. Today, it is embraced by many Jewish leaders, being seen as a salutary attempt to achieve a measure of understanding between religions, discerning similarities and differences through dialogue and close observation. However, the Ḥasid must go beyond such surface knowledge, seeking the spirit beneath the external forms and teachings, undertaking the more intrepid exploration of 'deep ecumenism,' in which one learns about *oneself* through participatory engagement with another religion or tradition.[18]

Judaism can no longer afford to see itself as the only valid religious tradition, or even as the most important. For such a view is ultimately self-defeating and destructive to the ecological system of the planet, which prefers diversity and depends on it for its own health. From this ecological perspective, every religion is like a vital organ of the planet; and for the planet's sake, each must remain healthy, functioning well in concert with the others for the good of the greater body. Thus, Jews must be the best and healthiest Jews they can be, doing their part in the planetary eco-system; but they must also do it in a way that recognizes the contributions of other religions and supports their healthy functioning as well.

Egalitarianism

As we embrace this larger 'organismic view,' seeing Judaism as a contributor to the health of the planetary system, we must not, as we have already said, forget to support the health and diversity of the internal Jewish ecological system. Judaism has, for too long, excluded women from full participation in the religious life of the community, denied the basic rights of individuals who are lesbian, gay, bisexual or transgendered, and erected high walls to protect Judaism from so-called 'outsiders.' Although there may have been times in our history when the exclusion of these groups served to preserve a fragile social order or seemed less important amid greater concerns for health and safety, today, their exclusion is untenable and acts like a cancer in the body of Judaism. If Judaism would be healed and give its best functioning back to the planet, it must embrace all of these groups. And in doing so, it will find that much of its new vitality and creativity will come directly from them.

Conclusion

But all of this is just a beginning. It is not definitive, not the final word, nor the only view of the matter. Our words are not 'the word' of the Fourth Turning of Hasidism. They are merely the product of a longing to serve God as deeply as our Hasidic ancestors once did, recognizing the needs of our time and attempting to call the future into the present with a name. It is only Hasidism itself—i.e., making ourselves transparent to God's grace and will, and living in the authentic presence of God—that can do the rest.

A Rebbe's Soul,
A Hasid's Yearning*

A Dialogue between Netanel Miles-Yépez
& Zalman Schachter-Shalomi on the
Vocation of a Rebbe

NETANEL MILES-YÉPEZ: Before we talk about anything else,
I want to ask you—What is a *rebbe?*

Zalman Schachter-Shalomi: A *rebbe* is a person whose soul
also includes the souls of their Ḥasidim. When a Ḥasid
comes to the *rebbe* with a problem, the *rebbe* attempts to
locate and connect with the soul of that Ḥasid as a part of
their own soul. And it is through the establishment of this
connection that the Ḥasid receives material and spiritual
benefit.

N.M-Y.: So a *rebbe* has the capacity and skill to find the soul
of another person *within*—a connection or resonance—
and to offer a particular help based on an attunement
to that resonance, one that is tailored to the Ḥasid's
particular needs, yes?

* This dialogue, which took place in Zalman Schachter-Shalomi's home in
Boulder, Colorado, was originally published in 2012 in his *The Geologist of the
Soul: Talks on Rebbe-craft and Spiritual Leadership.*

Z.S-S.: Yes, but not always to the same degree. It can depend on how much intrinsic connection there is between the soul of the *rebbe* and the particular Ḥasid. Rebbes have often sent potential Ḥasidim on in search of other guidance, because there is a sense that the *shoresh ha'neshamah,* the 'root of that person's soul,' may not be, as it were, housed with that particular *rebbe.* But if the Ḥasid belongs to the same *neshamah k'lalit,* 'general soul' or 'soul-cluster' as the *rebbe,* then the guidance may come easier and with more clarity.

That is not to say that the *rebbe* cannot function as a *rebbe* for others 'outside of his or her network,' but that there may be more ambiguity or obstacles to overcome because the context is different.

N.M-Y.: Because not only is there a particular soul-affinity between a *rebbe* and Ḥasid, being part of the same 'soul-cluster,' there is also a contract of intimacy between them, allowing for an unrestricted flow of information on different levels back and forth.

Z.S-S.: That's right. In the past, this was sometimes a formal contract, called a *k'tav hitkashrut,* a 'letter of self-binding' commitment to a *rebbe,* such as several Ḥasidim gave the Malakh, the Maggid's only son after the Maggid of Mezritch's passing; but mostly it was understood.[1] But whether written or not, the contract was clear.

N.M-Y.: A contract of intimacy and concern, and a contract to assist the Ḥasid in spiritual development?

Z.S-S.: Ideally. But, often, the people they were dealing with had more mundane concerns—children, the cows and the chickens. Some rebbes did what they could for whomever came to them, with whatever need. Others, like the Kotzker Rebbe, forbade people to come to them with concerns about their cows!

The ratio of spiritual to material concerns was perhaps best shown in a little anecdote about the Apter Rav, who got very excited when he got "a Ba'al Shemski *kvittel!*" That is to say, someone had brought him a prayer petition for a spiritual issue instead of the usual material prayer requests.

Of course, there were also rebbes who saw themselves like kings looking after the material and spiritual welfare of their Hasidim.[2] Nevertheless, the highest ideal in Hasidism was always to foster spiritual growth in Hasidim.

N.M-Y.: I find that I often have to explain the difference between a rabbi and *rebbe* to people who don't have a sense of what Hasidism is, or that there are normative and supra-normative approaches to Judaism. Given that we are talking about the *rebbe* as a model of Jewish spiritual leadership here, perhaps you might clarify the differences?

Z.S-S.: A rabbi in the past was a legal authority, empowered by his learning and other authorities to make decisions on what was kosher and what was not. But today, the idea of the rabbi is more fluid. The rabbi of today also leads the prayer service, gives sermons, teaches classes and counsels members of his or her congregation. In this way, today's rabbi functions more like a *rebbe*, but with an important distinction: the rabbi is still by-and-large a leader in an *external* sense, serving the Jewish needs of a community; the *rebbe*, on the other hand, is working with the deeper, *internal* needs of people with whom he or she is in an intimate guidance relationship.

N.M-Y.: I think it is also worth saying that, while one might become a rabbi by education, by studying in a *yeshiva* or going through an ordination program, one does not become a *rebbe* in the same way. While rabbis may be more or less skillful or talented, and have the same basic ordination, having demonstrated a certain mastery of information, a rebbe's mastery is not a mastery of *information*, but of *attunement.*

Z.S-S.: The rebbe's attunement is crucial. When I look at the original story of how the Ba'al Shem Tov challenged the Maggid of Mezritch to read and offer an explanation of a passage in Luria's *Eitz Ḥayyim*, I ask, "Why did the Maggid fail?" He offered a good explanation; it was all correct, a good head answer. In that, he was a good rabbi and good kabbalist in the knowledge sense. But he was not yet attuned to the reality beneath the words.[3]

All the Ba'al Shem Tov had to do was read and give over the same passage with attunement and the Maggid felt the reality beneath the words and became his disciple in order to learn how to do that himself. And he got it, and for several generations, he and his students were able to transmit that attunement to others. But attunement is not verbal, it's not left brain, so there is no way to write about that or get it through reading alone.

No, not everyone can become a *rebbe*, and certainly not by education; one needs something from *Above* to fullfil this mission.

N.M-Y.: You have often openly discussed the role and function of a *rebbe* as a model of spiritual leadership,[4] and I agree that it is necessary to do so; but I also feel the message might be misunderstood and play into our usual Western cultural dysfunction, seeing *rebbe*-hood as just another opportunity for the ego to shine, as a goal at the peak of Jewish spirituality. But *rebbe*-hood is so clearly not the goal, at least not in Hasidism. *The goal is to become a Hasid,* even for the *rebbe*.

In my eyes, *rebbe*-hood is a vocation, a role and a function to be fulfilled by those who are called to it, by those who cannot avoid it; but not a goal in itself. If anything, the *rebbe* is modeling how to be a *hasid,* with an open vertical connection, in a continuing relationship with their own *rebbe*, and especially with God.

Z.S-S.: That's right. The *rebbe* is still participating in a continuum of abasement like the Hasid, abasing the ego before *their own rebbe* (who may even have passed on), and most importantly, the Blessed and Holy One. The *rebbe* is fulfilling—what I would call today—a *temporary* vocational function for others; but is still, according to the ideal, intending only to be a Hasid.

This is what I was saying earlier about the *rebbe* being a symbol and a facilitator for the 'soul-cluster.' Take a light bulb as an example. The bulb itself cannot give off any light; it is simply a vehicle for the light. The electricity and light bulb source are actually from a power plant in some distant part of the city. But there must also be some resemblance in the bulb which enables it to receive power from the source—a wire, a contact—which connects it to the power source. Then, with the flip of a switch, the flow of electricity is opened, allowing the bulb to receive power and to function as a light bulb.

In the same way, the *rebbe* is not the Light, but its servant, receiving energy from God, the Power Source. And it is only by their own effacement and transparency that the Light shines through. The rebbe's real contribution to the process is in *serving* as a conduit—and here the metaphor breaks down a bit—in consciously recognizing the internal similarities and connections, and in knowing how to flip the switch.

N.M-Y.: Back when I used to assist you in teaching a class you called "Issues in Spiritual Direction," for people who were studying to be clergy, social workers, and transpersonal therapists at Naropa University, I noticed the same basic problem. There was a clear desire among many of them *to be* and *see themselves* as spiritual leaders, when many of them had never been led, never known what it was to be a disciple.

If someone has never been a disciple, it seems to me, there is a good possibility that they may not have the proper respect for a disciple.

Z.S-S.: When somebody wants to be a *rebbe*, without having served as a Ḥasid, it won't work. What makes a *rebbe* real is having spent time in the discipline of being a true disciple, of being a Ḥasid. The ego-reduction that has to happen to prepare someone for deep study, effective prayer, and for handling the responsibilities of *yeḥidut*, comes through conscious abasement to the preceptor, the *rebbe*, for the purpose of learning the rebbe's *attunement.*

Take the example of Reb Mordecai Yosef of Ishbitz, a great *rebbe* who had been a devoted Ḥasid. When he first came to Reb Simhah Bunim as a young man, he was not as tall as Reb Simhah Bunim. So Reb Simhah Bunim says, "Come, let's measure ourselves back-to-back." And when they had, he said, "Now I am taller than you; but you'll grow, and there will come a time when you are taller than I."

Reb Mordecai Yosef was a complete disciple to Reb Simhah Bunim. And later, he also submitted himself for an additional thirteen years to the Kotzker Rebbe, who had been the senior disciple of Reb Simhah Bunim. Toward the end of that time, the Kotzker Rebbe secluded himself more and more and gave over more responsibilities to Reb Mordecai Yosef. Indeed, he had put him in charge of the younger Ḥasidim. So, one day, when Reb Mordecai Yosef was about to depart from Kotzk, he went to give his regards to the Kotzker's son, Reb Dovid. Reb Dovid says to him, "Go in peace; but where is the *letzgelt,* some goodbye money?" (like paying your dues to the organization). So Reb Mordecai Yosef reaches into his pocket to take out some money; but when he pulls his hands out of his pockets, some *kvittlakh,* 'petitionary notes' from the Ḥasidim fall out on the ground. Reb Dovid, who sees this as a threat to his father's leadership says, "*Ah-h-h!* So you're taking *kvittlakh* already!" Reb Mordecai Yosef leans down, picks up the *kvittlakh,* stands and looks at Reb Dovid in the eye and says, "What do you think I came to learn from your father, to be a shoemaker?"

N.M-Y.: Reb Mordecai Yosef, the Ishbitzer, knows he has a vocation as a *rebbe,* and he knows because the people come to him.

Z.S-S.: And also because Reb Mendel, the Kotzker, had already entrusted him with responsibility for the younger Ḥasidim. Why else would he do that?

N.M-Y.: So the knowledge of the vocation comes both ways to him, from *below* and *above.* And when it is clear, he takes responsibility for learning how to do that well.

Z.S-S.: That's the point of how to become a *rebbe*: you *watch* and *observe.* It's the same situation we see with Reb Ahrele Roth and the Bluzhover Rebbe. The Bluzhover Rebbe says to his Ḥasidim, "You are all nice Ḥasidim, but this Hungarian boy watches everything I do to see what *yiḥud* I am making!"[5]

Reb Menachem Mendel, who became the seventh Lubavitcher Rebbe, kept journals in which he recorded what he saw and learned from Reb Yosef Yitzhak, the sixth Lubavitcher Rebbe. He was paying attention and watched with the right kind of eye.

At the same time, there are some people who, even if they don't have the vocation, are resting too much in the idea of being a Ḥasid, being a follower, and not really looking at how to make changes in their lives, not taking responsibility for their own situations. They like to hear and be near the *rebbe*, but not to watch close for how to make changes. That was what we saw with many Hasidic lineages who interpreted "The *tzaddik* lives by faith" (Hab. 2:4) as "The *tzaddik* gives life with his faith." So all the special spiritual work is for the *rebbe* alone, and not for the Ḥasid. The *rebbe* does it for you. That's an attitude we can't afford.

N.M-Y.: So this is the way in which the *rebbe* is a model for spiritual leadership; in modeling how to be a Ḥasid while in a leadership position, the *rebbe* provides an example of real service and humility, as well as a living frequency to which Ḥasidim and leaders of all types might attune themselves.

Z.S-S.: That "living frequency" is what is most important. You can tell someone how to do things, you can write a book about reading a *kvittel* or other shamanic things, but it's only words. You have to attune to a person who is actually doing it to really know what it is about.

N.M-Y.: A kind of intimate apprenticeship is necessary, where one learns both the external and internal qualities of how it is done by observation and feedback.

Z.S-S.: A person doesn't become a *rebbe* overnight, or without some checks. When my *rebbe*, Reb Yosef Yitzhak, was a young man, his father, the fifth Lubavitcher Rebbe, put him in charge of the *yeshiva*, and put him into a counseling position with the students. He would work with them and then bring both their issues and what he had recommended back to his father for refinement. It was a supervised process for him.

For years, I did this with the Rebbe, Reb Menachem Mendel, in *yeḥidut*, and through the letters I sent to him about what I was doing, and what I was recommending. And he would write back refinements and corrections. That feedback was critical to my development.

But I also want to say that there is lateral feedback that is also important. And this comes back to the issue of having been a Ḥasid before becoming a *rebbe*. If a person becomes a *rebbe* without having first been a Ḥasid *among Ḥasidim*—which has happened—there is something missing in their leadership.

N.M-Y.: You mean, without having experienced that fellowship, the common concerns, and the checks that come from spiritual friends?

Z.S-S.: It's important to have buddies, like Reb Dov Baer of Lubavitch said about having a spiritual companion: "That way, you have two *yetzer ha'tov*'s against one *yetzer ha'ra*"[6] Spiritual loners who have not come out of this kind of context, and yet who have become leaders, often don't have a respect for feedback.

Responsibility—*answerability*—is very important. I have seen talented, self-made people in *rebbe*-positions who didn't feel they were answerable to anyone, who thought that they were smarter and knew more than everyone, and so never checked anything out with anyone else. And I have seen others of this sort who were very, very good, but who had no feedback opening, and so would often talk and talk without reading the needs of the group. In this situation, the connection is lost, but they just continue talking.

It's so important to have a spiritual friend, or friends, to give you feedback, to laugh with and keep you from taking yourself too seriously. You don't get teased if you just become a *rebbe* without having been a Ḥasid.

N.M-Y.: We see that your *rebbe*, Reb Yosef Yitzhak, was *among* the Ḥasidim throughout his youth.

Z.S-S.: As a child, the older Ḥasidim were always around and they liked him.

N.M-Y.: And he talked to them and listened to their stories, and sat among them watching his father, a Ḥasid among Ḥasidim.

Z.S-S.: And that showed itself in the way he related to Ḥasidim later when he was a *rebbe*. In his talks, as was the case in his father's time, there would be dialogue with the Ḥasidim; it wasn't just a one-way thing. He was really listening to them and their concerns.

Did you get to see the documentary, *Kumaré*, about the young Indian-American filmmaker who fakes an Indian accent and pretends to be an authentic *guru* in Arizona?[7]

N.M-Y.: I did. It was amazing—both in its illustration of our cultural dysfunctionality around spirituality, and in the authentic teachings that managed to come through.

Z.S-S.: You saw how things changed? How he switched from mockery because he found himself actually listening to the people who came to him?

N.M-Y.: Yes, and you could see exactly when the switch occurred: the moment he felt the weight of what was being brought to him—the heavy things people were dealing with—and how they expected answers from him that would actually work. Then he began to understand what a responsibility it is to be a spiritual leader. No one who doesn't listen, and who doesn't feel that burden should be offering advice.

Z.S-S.: Another thing I want to say about being "a Ḥasid among Ḥasidim" is about the training that happens there with mentors. As much contact as I had with the sixth and seventh rebbes of Lubavitch, I had more with my *mashpiyyim,* with my 'mentors' who were senior Ḥasidim of the Rebbe, especially in my youth. These were venerable Ḥasidim like Reb Yisroel Jacobson, Reb Eliya Simpson, Reb Shmuel Levitin, and Reb Avraham Pariz.

We need to emphasize these relationships in our situation as well. We need more *mashpiyyim* who are good adepts and guides to mentor others, and more people to actively seek them out. It can't all depend on a single person, on a *rebbe,* who is supposed to do everything. The *rebbe* needs a lot of support staff.

Remember the story about the Ba'al Shem Tov and the ladder?

N.M-Y.: When the Ba'al Shem Tov was praying and saw himself as climbing a scaffold of Ḥasidim to reach the golden bird in the top of the tree?[8]

Z.S-S.: And just as he is about to reach it, the scaffold collapses! While he was praying, the Ḥasidim had gotten tired and had gone home. You see, he couldn't do it without them, and they didn't understand their role in the work that was being done.

When I was leading retreats at Fellowship House and Farm in Pennsylvania, often I had to be both the *rebbe* and the *shammes,* putting out chairs, distributing papers, and arranging everything. No one was supporting me; and yet, people came up to me while I was doing these things and expected me to function like a *rebbe* for them! How could I be in that mind-space when I had to do these things? You cannot function as the *rebbe* when you are setting up the tables and chairs. If someone wants *yehidut*, I would say, "Let me prepare and get into that place first."

Look, if I had to do all that you and others are doing for me at this point in my life, I would never even get a chance to say, 'Hello, God.' For a *rebbe* to function, there needs to be three or four people supporting them in that work.

N.M-Y.: That's a good way of looking at the whole situation: there is no *rebbe* without Ḥasidim; and without the people supporting the *rebbe*-function, *there is no rebbe-function at all.*

Z.S-S.: And we need that function, and the wisdom of how to do it, to continue to help us map our future.

Do you remember the story of Reb Elimelekh of Lizhensk and the Seer of Lublin, about the *rebbe*'s 'event horizon'?[9] It shows us that there is some overlap necessary, disciples who can take up the reins in the *rebbe*'s lifetime, because there are things coming up that impact the next generation that the *rebbe* before doesn't handle; they may contribute a piece to it, but it is not entirely theirs to take on. So the work must be continued by the rebbes that follow.

Matisyahu
& the New T'shuvah[*]

SOMETIME BACK, A good friend got me to listen to Matisyahu for the first time . . . and I've been a little dissatisfied with other music ever since.

Initially, I was reluctant to listen to his music at all. Not because I didn't think he was good. I had heard a sample of him while strolling through a store one day and stopped to listen. He definitely had something; but I wasn't interested in being caught by the marketing. Obviously, the contrast of a bearded Jew in the 'uniform' of a Lubavitcher Ḥasid—black fedora, loose black suit and open-collared white shirt—with first-rate rap and reggae talent is a marketing opportunity few labels could refuse. But being rebellious by nature, anything I have 'simply got to hear,' I tend to avoid as long as I possibly can, or at least until I've forgotten I was avoiding it. So by the time my friend lent me Matisyahu's first major studio album, *Youth*, the album had already been out for four years, and his follow-up album, *Light*, for four months.

Nevertheless, for friendship's sake, I put it on one day and listened to it while I worked. When it was finished, I uttered a grudgingly respectful "It's good." Then I

---

[*] Originally published in *Spectrum: A Journal of Renewal Spirituality* on September 6th, 2012 after the release of Matisyahu's album *Spark Seeker.*

listened to it again . . . *and again*. . . *and again*. I just couldn't stop playing it.

My mind was starting to catch-up with the lyrics and I realized suddenly that I had found something I'd been longing for . . . music that was as satisfying to me *spiritually* as it was emotionally and aesthetically. Until that moment, I almost had to 'flip a switch' inside, or wait for the right mood to strike, if I was going to listen to so-called 'spiritual music' (which is a little embarrassing, as I am considered a spiritual teacher and am the author of books on Hasidic spirituality).

It's not that I don't love the traditional Hasidic *niggunim*—the sometimes contemplative, sometimes rousing melodies—I learned from my *rebbe*, my teacher; but they belong to a heart and mind-space I associate with prayer and Hasidic gatherings, and come from a time and a Jewish *shtetl*-culture which is not my own.

In my mind's eye, I can see the holy Ba'al Shem Tov, the founder of Hasidism, singing these melodies as he walked to the market on weekdays or attuned his disciples to the right 'frequency' during a *tish*, for they were both *sacred* and *contemporary* for him. And yet, for me, they are only sacred. Of course, one occasionally drifts into my mind while I'm out for walk; but, for the most part, that territory is owned by the music I grew up with, the music of modern culture that speaks to my senses and my aesthetics today.

But listening to Matisyahu's unique fusion of spiritually influenced lyrics, his raw and refined hip-hop reggae rhythms alternating, gave me something I'd been missing: it brought the separate worlds of my secular and sacred consciousness together.

Before him, I had listened to music always looking for deeper expressions of human love and possibility, often reading spiritual themes into it; but once I found something that accomplished that for me, I almost didn't want to hear anything else. I wanted Katy Perry and P!nk to sing about ecstatic union; Aimee Mann to sing about *m'rirut,* 'bitterness of heart'; Eric Hutchinson to sing about *simḥah,* 'joy' and sweetness; Coldplay and Citizen Cope about storming the gates of heaven! Thank God for Trevor Hall's *bhakti* devotionalism, MC Yogi's "Give Love" and Damian Marley's "Road to Zion." I think I'd have starved otherwise, or gone into withdrawal. Once you've had a taste of what you always wanted, there's no going back.

The Returnees and a New Jewish Art

When I was a teenager and first beginning to write and paint seriously, I read books on Michelangelo and Tolstoy, and wondered at the fact that there was so little spirituality represented in great art today. After the Renaissance, it seemed, the best artists—with a few notable exceptions—had abandoned Judaism and Christianity (not without some justification) and had thrown themselves headlong into a purely secular world of personal expression. In their absence, the art of religion and spirituality had become increasingly ossified and outdated. Even worse for me were the overtly religious attempts to contemporize religious art by 'hacks' and third-rate talent. These anemic experiments with 'spiritualizing the contemporary' only emphasized the poor quality of the art and the absence of truly powerful and inspiring messages in it. Clearly, what we needed was a spirituality that could draw the best artists back to religion, one that would feed their creativity instead of inhibiting it.

While the evolving marketplace of religion and spirituality today can be overwhelming and distracting, it also gives us a new freedom and new options for spiritual practice that did not exist in the past, or at least not for a long time. Sometimes this makes it harder to settle into a discipline; but it is also perfect for the spiritual aspirant ready to take responsibility for their own spiritual path, ready to replace authority imposed from the outside for a higher standard of personal authenticity on the inside. In Judaism, this is especially clear in the various manifestations of what is often called, 'neo-Hasidism,' inspired by the music and teachings of Rabbi Shlomo Carlebach and Rabbi Zalman Schachter-Shalomi.

But the inspiration for Jewish artists today isn't only coming from the radical left; it is also coming from progressive and spiritually open parts of traditional Hasidism as well, especially from the lineages of Bratzlav and Ḥabad (sometimes Breslov and Chabad). Although Ḥabad-Lubavitch Hasidism is often lumped in a category of rigid ultra-Orthodoxy, it is nevertheless a tradition with deep roots in mystical spirituality, with teachers profoundly committed to serving Jews everywhere.

At a time when he needed it, it provided a younger Matthew Miller (later Matisyahu) with shelter and a way to return to Judaism. And to its credit, this so-called 'old tradition' found a way to encourage him to express his love of God through the contemporary music that had most resonance with his soul.

And yet, this is only a return in our time to what was well-known in the early years of Hasidism and throughout Jewish history, i.e., that our music was taken from the landscapes and cultures all around us. Thus, Russian Hasidic lineages have melodies that sound distinctly Russian, and Polish Ḥasidim have melodies that sound Polish. The great Hasidic master, Rebbe Nahman of Bratzlav speaks of how the glory of God calls forth even from the stories and melodies of the non-Jews.[1] And we hear of how the great Hungarian Hasidic master and composer, Eisik of Kalev—"a soul from the Temple of Music"—used to go out and listen to the songs and melodies of the Hungarian shepherds. There is even a story of how he purchased a love song he heard from a wandering 'Gypsy' (Rom, one of the Roma) and adapted the words to speak of God and the *Shekhinah*, the feminine presence of divinity.[2]

Today, a kid from a culturally Jewish home in White Plains might just as easily be exposed to the reggae of Bob Marley as a young woman in South Carolina to the Dixie Chicks, or someone else in California to the updated *rancheras* of Lila Downs. How is this any different from what happened in the past? It's the way it should be.

We know from the biological sciences that any closed system tends to degenerate. It needs a fresh infusion of DNA from outside to create a healthy system; which is to say, *life wants diversity*, and gets it one way or another. Hasidism, and Judaism generally, are getting it through the 'returnees,' from the Jews who have wandered out into the wider world, sampling its art and music, the spirituality and meditation of other cultures, who have come back 'infected' with these foreign elements, elements which in time will create a healthier Judaism.

It is a reciprocal relationship based on permeability: the more open and deeply integrated elements of Judaism are making a way for cultural and disaffected Jews to return; and as they do, they are bringing with them what Judaism needs for the future.

Breaking Our Idols

Nevertheless, there is a kind of 'all or nothing' attitude that continues to plague Jewish identity. This summer I was talking to a man at a Jewish Festival who said to me: "I'm trying to learn *'real'* Judaism now; so I'm studying a commentary by the Lubavitcher Rebbe. I don't want to read about *'made-up'* Judaism."

I didn't argue with him, but I looked the man up and down and saw a lawyer or businessman in his 50s—no beard, no *tzitzit*—who probably didn't wear *t'fillin* when he prayed, and probably wouldn't ever do any of these things in a serious way (as they would interfere with the life he knew and had created for himself). And this wasn't a problem for me; but I wondered why a man like this—who had made different choices and wasn't likely to change— was so certain that Orthodox Hasidic Judaism was the only "real Judaism"? After all, it's all *"made-up"* Judaism. There are no Jewish practitioners of the original religion handed down to the *Ivri'im*, the 'Hebrews' at Mount Sinai. The Juda-*isms* that we know today are all the result of evolution. But so many Jews across the spectrum— whether they choose to live that lifestyle or not, or even whether they like it or not—continue to see one version of Judaism, Orthodoxy, as *the* version of Judaism.

There are reasons for this, certainly. One good reason is that Orthodox Judaism maintains the maximum of Jewish tradition, and thus appears to be Judaism to the *'nth degree.'* So anything less seems to be 'less Jewish.' But even as I laud the preservation of these traditions, and support my holy friends in the Hasidic community, I cannot say that this Judaism is any more valid than another. It may be more richly imbued with traditional Jewish knowledge and external symbol, but is it necessarily richer in inner experience? *Maybe* . . . but not by any necessity.

If there is a deficiency of passion or fervor, of love or longing for God and commitment in liberal Judaism, or any other form of Jewish observance, the problem is where it has always been—in the heart of the individual.

Today, liberal Jews need to ask themselves: 'Am I embarrassed to love God openly because I am an academic or a professional? Am I ashamed to pray with fervor because my friends don't, or because my neighbors are not Jewish?' What does this have to do with Orthodoxy? This is the real challenge of modern Judaism: to live a Jewish life, according to whatever definition you might want to use, as if it really mattered.

Allowing for Evolution

In the years since the live version of "King Without a Crown" first broke into the Top 10, both Matisyahu and his music have gone through a lot of changes. And, as a result, his popularity has soared, passing well beyond the confines of the Jewish world (especially when his popular anthem "One Day" was played at the Olympic Games). And yet, as he has become more successful, he has also received more criticism from fans.

In the winter of 2011, before kicking-off his "Festival of Light" tour in New York, Matisyahu shaved off his signature beard, causing many Jewish fans to question whether he was still a 'good Jew.'[3] And with the release of his album, *Spark Seeker,* many of his non-Jewish fans have begun to question whether he is still a 'reggae artist,' or whether he has defected to the 'pop' scene.

I have to say, I've listened to all of these identity discussions with some disappointment; it's clear that they say more about *us* than they do about him. For all of his fans, across the spectrum, he was unquestionably a 'good Jew' when he wore the clothes of a Lubavitcher Ḥasid. And though there was some grumbling from the more conservative elements when he abandoned the 'uniform,' opting for a more contemporary and relaxed look (similar to that of a young American-style Bratzlaver Ḥasid), he was still clearly a 'religious Jew.' After all, he kept his side curls *(peyot)* and beard, and still allowed his ritual fringes *(tzitzit)* to hang loose.

But when he chose to break out of the box, removing some of these externals, Jewish fans—*of all levels of Jewish observance*—acted as if they had been personally betrayed. It was as if he represented Judaism for them by his embrace of these external Jewish symbols, whether *they* wore them themselves or not! This is something we need to come to terms with as Jews.

When I first started listening to early Matisyahu albums like *Shake Off the Dust... Arise* and *Live at Stubb's,* the influence of Ḥabad Ḥasidism was obvious, even explicit in lyrics like, "We want *Moshiach* now!" The lyrics were also very linear, discursive and mission-oriented, like the current version of Ḥabad (Chabad) Ḥasidism itself. But with the album *Youth*, I could already sense a small shift toward Bratzlav Hasidism. And by the time *Light* was released, the influence of Rebbe Nahman of Bratzlav was explicit. The lyrics were far more intuitive and drew from the imagery of Rebbe Nahman's teachings and stories, alluding to "the lost princess" and the "seven beggars."

So when Matisyahu announced that his new album, *Spark Seeker*, would be themed around the Ba'al Shem Tov, the founder of Hasidism himself, I was not surprised in the least, and suspected there would be more changes ahead. There was even a sense of 'homecoming' about the announcement.

For a Ḥasid, going back to the Ba'al Shem Tov is a return to the source of Hasidism. It's a 'radical' act, in the sense of the word's original meaning, 'to go back to the root.' In this case, it is a return to the inherent joy of service to God and an overflowing of love toward others.

A person doesn't seek out the Ba'al Shem Tov to visit the 'archives' of Hasidism, or the 'museum' of the original Hasidic cultural forms, but to dip naked in the *mikveh*, the ritual bath of the original Hasidic spirit, removing all the forms, all the appearances, all the clothing and accretions that have built up over time that come between us and that spirit, between us and God. And having dipped there, we re-dress, redress the balance, remedy and set right our relationship to God. Thus, to me, it is no more surprising that a Jew with a beard might choose to shave it after re-attuning to the spirit of the Ba'al Shem Tov than to see another without a beard choose to grow one afterward. Both acts indicate 'renewal.'

A successful artist can so easily become a prisoner of their own success. But Matisyahu has become successful in a way that has threatened to cage him twice over: if he shifts his Jewish identity and changes the iconic image that made him famous, he threatens to alienate his Jewish fans who somehow feel dependent on that particular image; if he allows his music to evolve along its natural course, he risks losing those fans who only want to think of him as a 'reggae artist.' The projections are too heavy, too limiting, and too banal to bear. A person cannot be a symbol anymore than an artist can be a genre . . . but they can create both if they are allowed to.

Everybody that falls in love with an album or a song wants to have that artist repeat it over and over again in slightly different versions. But that's not how the art works. It evolves according to its own mysterious destiny. It wants to grow, to change and find new paths. And so does the artist. Once somebody challenged Gandhi about things he had said and done in the past, saying that he was now contradicting himself. He replied simply, "Yes, that's what I believed yesterday. But this is who I am today."[4]

I don't really know anything about Matisyahu other than I love his music. I don't think he's a *tzaddik*, a saint, nor a Jewish icon to be celebrated by kids, or to make us feel good about being Jews. What he appears to be now is a man trying to be a Ḥasid from the inside out. And I suppose, like many of us, he feels that he is failing at it much of the time. What really matters is the *trying*. I think 'becoming religious' was 'trying.' Singing a Hasidic *niggun* with a reggae flavor was also 'trying.' But removing a successful persona when you realize it has become a mask is more than 'trying'—it's *bravery,* because to remove it is to risk losing everything. Evolution is bravery.

As I look at Matisyahu's evolution from black-hatted Lubavitcher to a beardless bleach-blond, I don't see a man forsaking his commitment to Judaism, but a man turning from a life lived from the *outside-in* to one lived from the *inside-out.* And 'turning' it inside-out is the new *t'shuvah.* *

---

* *T'shuvah* is Hebrew for 'turning,' and is usually used to refer to 'repentance,' 'returning' or turning back to God.

The Miracle of Re-Dedication[*]

A *D'rash* on Ḥannukah from
Netanel Miles-Yépez & Matisyahu Miller

Oᴜʀ ᴄᴜʀʀᴇɴᴛ ᴛʀᴏᴜʙʟᴇꜱ remind us that the kinds of troubles and conflicts we find in the Ḥannukah story are not just a thing of the past; they're not 'history' for us, but a reality to which we can actually relate.[1] Just as there were wars and troubles in that time, there are wars and troubles today—natural disasters and personal catastrophes that make a mess of our lives. But this is not the message of Ḥannukah, 'that bad things happened to us then, and continue to happen to us now.' The message of Ḥannukah is that miracles occurred at that time, and also occur in our lives today.

What was the real miracle of Ḥannukah? Some people say it was that a little band of Jewish rebels managed to defeat a numerically superior army of Greeks, an army that had taken over their land and desecrated their Holy Temple. Others say it was the miracle of the oil: that the last little cruse of ritually prepared oil somehow lasted for the entire eight days it would take to make new

* Originally published in *The Huffington Post*, December 10ᵗʰ, 2012. After the publication of the article "Matisyahu and the New T'shuvah," Matisyahu contacted the author about collaborating on a Ḥannukah article that would promote a new song, "Happy Hanukkah" the proceeds of which would be donated to victims of Hurricane Sandy.

oil for the Temple *menorah*. But maybe, *just maybe,* the real miracle was the 'miracle of re-dedication,' of starting over and starting again.

The Hebrew word *ḥannuk,* means 'to dedicate.' And when we use the word *ḥannukah,* we are really talking about the 're-dedication' of the Temple after it had been desecrated, and about the 're-dedicating' of our lives to a relationship with the source of all. So when our forbears decided to call the holiday Ḥannukah, it is clear that they wanted to emphasize the aspect of it that has to do with 'starting again.'

But what is so miraculous about starting again and re-dedicating ourselves to something? The answer is: *it represents something indestructible in us,* something that hopes against hope, that gets up when all the evidence says that we'll probably just get knocked down again later. To live inspired by hope is a true miracle in our world.

Sometimes the message about 're-dedication' gets lost amid all the other themes of Ḥannukah, amid all the dreidel-spinning parties filled with latkes and doughnuts. But if we really think about it, 're-dedication' makes Ḥannukah one of the most personal of the Jewish holidays. After all, who hasn't had to pick up the pieces of their lives? It doesn't take a hurricane or a missile to make a mess of them. Often, we do a pretty good job of it ourselves. And when we are sitting there, amid all the rubble and ruin of it, we have to make a decision: will we get up and start again, or will we just lie down?

All the miracles of the Ḥannukah story start when Judah Maccabee and his followers decided to get up and fight back, when they decided to re-take the Temple and clean it up, and when they made the decision to re-light the Temple *menorah* with the oil they had, instead of waiting until they could make more.[2]

All it takes is a little light, a little hope to get started. Every year, Ḥannukah comes around the Winter Solstice, at the darkest point of the year, when we are often feeling most tired and most hopeless. But it is also at this point that things begin to change, and the light begins to increase, little-by-little, like the candles in the *menorah*.[3]

There is a very deep teaching in the Jewish mystical tradition that we need to remember in our darkest hours: just as the Jews who cleaned the Temple found one little cruse of oil to burn amid all the wreckage, all of us have a *yeḥidah*, 'a tiny point' in our souls that is always pure and in contact with God, no matter how much the rest of us feels broken and desolate. There is always something—a little spark of divinity, a little oil to make a ray of light to shine in the darkness—something we can take hold of and use to re-build our lives.

On Ḥannukah, we remember that holy point within us, that little light that is always pure, that gives us a hope that we can share with everyone around us. We practice the miracle of re-dedicating ourselves to a purpose, whether it be to helping others re-build their own lives, or to starting again in ours, because that's the true source of the happiness of Ḥannukah.

PART IV
*Problems and Perspectives
on the Spiritual Path*

The Other Side of Fear*

By THE TIME I was thirteen, I had become deathly afraid of speaking in public. Before that, I'm sure I had fairly ordinary fears about it; but I was able to do it, and was even a little proud of the ability. By thirteen, however, the very thought of it was enough to cause a panic attack. My heart would beat wildly in my chest. I would break out in a cold sweat and become dizzy. My anxiety was so intense, I didn't know if I would survive it. I felt as if I might collapse or go entirely blank, which seemed equally terrible. And what would happen then? *Death? Derision?* I couldn't think beyond the fear.

Looking back, I wonder if the biological changes of puberty had somehow catalyzed an earlier trauma and caused me to shy away from attention. Whatever the cause, I had a serious problem and soon began to make excuses to avoid speaking at school. I skipped classes for days at a time so that it wouldn't look as if I was only missing the days I was required to read or give a presentation.

Not surprisingly, my grades dropped; but as I had always been quiet, and wasn't generally considered very smart or a good student, no one seemed to think it a cause for great concern.

---

* This article was first published in *Spectrum: A Journal of Renewal Spirituality,* August 25th, 2013.

Once, in high school, I had an English teacher who was kind and encouraging, and I thought I might try to face my fears in her class. Part of me wanted someone to recognize that I wasn't really as dumb or timid as people thought. She had asked us to memorize a short passage from a book or play and to recite it for the class. As I was then beginning to read Shakespeare, I decided to memorize a monologue from his *Julius Caesar* (part of which I can still recite to this day). Looking at it now, it is interesting how often the word 'fear' is mentioned. "I rather tell thee what is to be fear'd than what I fear."[1] Maybe I wished that I could speak so openly of my own fears. I certainly hoped that I would give this speech and be rid of them.

The night before, I rehearsed every word perfectly. I was amazed at what I understood and how I could evoke the drama in the words. I even felt a momentary sense of triumph . . . Then, as if in response, I was seized with terror. Fear gripped my heart and I knew I would never do it. In despair, I punched a hole in the living room wall and slumped to the floor, sobbing. The next day, I acted blasé when called upon and pretended that I hadn't bothered to do the assignment, casually accepting the failing grade as if it were unimportant to me.

Needless to say, I barely graduated high school.

Although I had enrolled in community college after graduation, I quickly withdrew after just a few classes. I didn't know what I wanted to do, and there really wasn't any money for it. So I got a job in a bookstore and began to spend all of my free time reading and painting.

After a few years of working, it became clear that I wanted to study religion and philosophy. And I now had another reason to go back to school: I had fallen in love, and my fiancée was about to transfer to a university. So we got married and I enrolled in a community college in the same city. But I continued to avoid public speaking. Throughout my time at Lansing Community College, and later at Michigan State University, I managed to keep my head down and avoid talking. My grades were good, but I still trembled at the thought of being called upon in class, or even having to make a comment on anything.

It wasn't until grad school that things began to change.

The Naropa Process

In 1998, I applied to enter a master's program at the Naropa Institute in Boulder, Colorado. The program stressed "engagement" and a "process-orientation" that let me know it would not be easy to hide my fear of public speaking. Nevertheless, I was determined to go. I decided to take it as a challenge (though, somewhere in the back of my mind, I'm sure I thought that I might just be wily enough to avoid any "processing" out loud). If I actually thought that, I couldn't have been more wrong.

During the two-day orientation, there was a luncheon at which we introduced ourselves to the people at our table; then a support group meeting of 7-10 individuals from the incoming class to which we had to introduce ourselves at length again; and then a meeting of 20 or so new students in the major at which which we had to talk about what had brought us to Naropa.

Somehow, I got through all of this tolerably well and was just beginning to relax a little when I entered

Shambhala Hall for a last session with all the incoming students. We sat down in a large circle, perhaps 60 to 100 of us. Then a microphone was brought out and handed to a student directly across from me in the circle. Immediately, I felt the panic set-in. We were asked to say "a few words" about what we hoped to take away from our experience at Naropa.

The long semi-circular journey of the microphone to the place where I was sitting felt like an eternity in Hell. Desperately, I tried to think of what I might say; but nothing came. I thought I might die.

Finally, as the microphone made its way to the person sitting immediately to my right, I heard a voice whisper inside my head—*"just tell the truth."*

It was clear that personal disclosures were honored at Naropa, and although I wasn't terribly comfortable with the idea, I decided it was time to 'out myself.' The microphone was passed to me. Nervously, I took it and looked around at the blank faces staring at me. Then, somewhat tremulously, I said: "I have to admit . . . *I'm terrified.* I've always been afraid of speaking in public; but I think this is what I've come here for—to challenge myself, and to explore new territory. I look forward to doing that with all of you."

Almost immediately, I felt an upswell of support from everyone in the room. A wave of compassion rolled over me. It had worked. By admitting my fear, I had bypassed all the judgments that might be made about my obvious nervousness (especially if I had pretended it didn't exist and stuttered my way through a pathetic introduction).

It was my first real success and was followed by many smaller ones in the days to come. Naropa simply is not a place where you can avoid speaking up. In one venue or another, you are going to have to talk. Gradually, I got somewhat used to it. At first, I mentioned my 'problem' whenever I had to speak in class; but it wasn't long before I was able give up that particular crutch as well. It just wasn't necessary anymore.

As graduation approached, just under two years later, I was asked to give a guest lecture in another department. It was an art history class focusing on South Asian art. As I was then considered a minor authority on Hindu iconography, I was asked to give a talk to the art students. Immediately, the fears came up again and I hesitated. I was fairly certain I could do it, but it was a new situation for me and I was afraid. Finally, I agreed, and a week later found myself sitting on a stool and giving an hour and a half talk about the famous Shiva Nataraja icon of Hinduism. The students seemed appreciative and I left relieved. What I didn't know then was that just a few days later, I would face a much more difficult test. In fact, it was quite literally a test: it was my last exam at Naropa.

The Warrior Exam

Now, if you've never heard of Naropa, then you need to know something about its founder and how things work there. Chögyam Trungpa Rinpoche (1939-1987) was one of the earliest and most significant Tibetan Buddhist masters to teach Buddhism in America. He was also one of the most radical. Not content with simply transplanting Tibetan Buddhist cultural and religious forms in American soil, he actually wanted to create a new fusion of East and West, blending the best aspects of education in each. Thus he founded the Naropa Institute in 1974, which eventually became the first accredited "Buddhist-inspired" academic institution in the United States.

At Naropa, you could find a recognizable version of university academics, but often presented in a different context. Instead of sitting in rows of desks or at tables, we sat in circles—sometimes on chairs, sometimes on cushions—and began each class with a respectful bow toward the center of the circle and each other. We also studied different academic subjects, some of them represented perhaps for the first time in the West. We studied Buddhist texts and philosophical schools, and even had a class called "Meditation Practicum." And in some of these classes, we were required to take what were called "warrior exams."

The warrior exam is based on the Tibetan Buddhist debate tradition, which resembles a kind of ritualized intellectual combat. In it, the 'defender' sits amid a circle of Buddhist monks or nuns and fields questions from an intellectual challenger or 'attacker,' standing before them. Each question or 'attack' is accompanied by gestures that suggest the stringing of a bow and the shooting of an arrow. The defender only departs the field of combat when the attacker catches them in a contradiction, a stalemate is declared, or the attacker is sufficiently satisfied with the defender's answer. From this tradition, Chögyam Trungpa developed the warrior exam, believing that there was something in it that might evoke the deepest 'warrior' qualities of the person being questioned. He also saw it as a container in which a psychological transformation might be accomplished. That is to say, it was meant to be a place for a person to face their fears.

After almost two years at Naropa, I had been through a number of warrior exams in fairly intimate classroom settings and no longer had much fear of them. In fact, I was becoming so comfortable with them by the time I graduated that I barely gave them a second thought. So as I entered the little cottage classroom for my final warrior exam on my last day at Naropa, I was unconcerned.

We had been given the questions to review the week before. This is usually a sheet of 10 to 15 two-part questions, some of which are fairly simple, and some quite difficult. Since you don't know which question you will get, you have to study for all of them and prepare oral answers for each. Well, I had glanced at the questions when I got them, and seeing that I knew the answers, never thought to look at them again. It was not a particularly difficult class and I thought it would be a breeze.

During a Naropa warrior exam, the class sits on the floor in a circle, often with each individual on a Japanese meditation cushion called a *zafu*, which is itself placed on a larger flat cushion called a *zabuton*. In the center of the circle are two sets of cushions facing one another with two bowls between them. In one bowl are folded slips of paper on which are written the names of all the students. In the other bowl are the questions.

First, the name of a questioner is selected, after which the questioner draws the name of a person to be examined. The examinee then selects a question from the other bowl. If they are happy with that question, they will then hand it to the questioner so that it may be read aloud to the class. If for some reason they would prefer to answer a different question, they may reach into the bowl again. However, this question *must be* answered. After it is read aloud, the examinee answers all parts of the question to the best of their ability, with as much detail as possible. When they are finished, the questioner may ask a follow-up question, or may signal their satisfaction with the answer. Then the instructor or other students may ask their own questions until they too are satisfied with the examinee's understanding. If they are, the examination is over and the two persons in the center bow to one another.

After a couple of rounds like this, my name is selected from the bowl. I step into the circle and sit down opposite my questioner. We bow to one another and I calmly reach into the bowl for my question. I pull out a little white strip of paper, unfold it, and to my surprise . . . *I cannot think of the answer.*

"No matter," I think, putting it aside to draw another question. I unfold the new slip of paper, and to my horror . . . *I find that I cannot think of the answer to this question either!*

I can feel the blood rushing into my face and the beginnings of moisture on my forehead. I look down for a moment, and then hand the paper resignedly to my questioner who reads the question out loud. There is a moment of silence before I say, *"I don't know."*

I can see the surprised looks on the faces of my classmates. By this time, I had acquired a reputation for being one of the more 'bookish' persons at Naropa, and I was commonly thought to 'have all the answers.' But in this moment, I have none, and I actually see my questioner's mouth drop open a little when I say it.

Feeling the panic rising, I make a decision.

Inside, I know I have the answers to these questions; I just can't seem to access them. I think to myself, "I'm not going to fail this exam just because I'm having a memory lapse!" I'm determined to give some kind of an answer.

Into the already tense silence, I finally speak up: "I honestly can't think of the answer. I know it's in me, somewhere; I'm just drawing a complete blank. So . . . *I want to ask a favor* . . . If you'll hang in there with me, I want to try and talk my way through the question until I find the answer."

I look at my questioner. Unsure of what to do, she looks at the instructor who calmly nods his assent.

Making myself as calm as possible, I say, "Please read me the question again." She reads it again and I repeat the first part aloud. Then I start to take all the words apart, thinking out loud and passing through all the Buddhist concepts to which this might refer, giving brief definitions of each and dismissing them all one by one.

Then I begin to look at how I might answer the question without reference to Buddhism or the specific text to which the question refers. Still, I haven't got it. I'm missing something. I ask my questioner to read the second part of the question. I listen intently and go through the same long, fruitless process.

Then, suddenly, it comes to me. Everything I have temporarily forgotten floods back into my mind and I can feel my face lighting up. Everyone knows 'I have it.' The relief in the room is palpable. I build on my earlier explorations and give the most thorough answer I can possibly give. I explore parallel concepts, give the arguments for and against the position and paraphrase the words of the text . . . For a moment, I even consider giving the page numbers of the answers in the text, but figure that this would be showing off. After faltering so badly in the beginning, however, I don't want to leave even the slightest doubt that I know and understand the answer thoroughly!

When I finish, I look at my questioner. She says with a smile, "I'm satisfied." I then look to the instructor and my classmates who all nod their satisfaction. Then someone begins to clap and the others join in until the whole class is clapping. I bow to my questioner and take her place as questioner for the next student.

In that moment, I knew that a significant chapter in my life had come to a close. This was the situation I had always feared, that I would come up short, panic, go blank and prove that all my personal fears about myself were true.

It had actually happened. But something else had happened that I had not anticipated. *I had lived.* I didn't collapse and the world didn't stop. I had forgotten what I knew, certainly! But I was still there and able to make decisions about what to do next and how I felt about what was happening to me. That was the power I had left to me.

I realized then that we don't often look beyond the terrible moments we fear. We almost never ask ourselves, 'What is on the 'other side' of this fear?' We tend to think that this is where the story ends—'fade to black.' But my story hadn't ended. I was still alive and could still act on my own behalf. In many ways, I was now free. My fears were realized and my world had not come to an end. It isn't pretty, but when the worst has already happened to you, what more is there to fear? So I asked myself, 'What comes next?' And the only answer I wanted to give was, 'No more running.'

In the years that followed, I was asked more and more frequently to give talks on particular aspects of religion to local groups or at different colleges. And in doing so, I discovered that I had something of a vocation as a teacher and a gift for public speaking.

Still, there were many times when the old panic got hold of me just before a talk and I would have to remember that I had already lived through the worst. On other occasions, I had to deal with different permutations of the fear; for instance, that I would give a 'bad talk.'

One night, forced to give a presentation for work on a subject in which I had little interest, I gave a very poor performance. The next day, I said to a dear friend who had been there, "That was pretty bad, wasn't it?" With the characteristic directness of an Israeli, she said, *"Yes, it was."* I laughed out loud. She was right. It was terrible; but somehow I felt okay about it because I had now survived that fear as well.

Today, I still feel nervous before speaking to a group, especially if I am caught off guard or find myself in a new situation. But I am no longer embarrassed or ashamed of the fact. I am aware of the momentary tremor and simply accept it. I tell myself, *"I belong in this moment,"* and then I ask the question on the other side of the fear, "What comes next?" And there is always an answer.

What's Happiness
Got to Do With It?*

"I'M STRUGGLING WITH LIVING."

It was not an appeal for my pity. It was a simple statement, trembling on his vocal chords, and tightening something in my chest when I heard it. *Truth . . .* It felt *true*.

He paused a moment, and I wondered then how many people have felt this particular feeling through the millennia of human experience. What strange animals we are that we struggle "with living." Not that we struggle *for life* or *in life*, like all creatures, but that human beings actually struggle *with living*. Is there another animal that does that?

He had called me, like many others, because I'm supposed to have the answers, spiritual prescriptions that can solve such maladies. But on that day, I had to confess—*"I'm struggling with living, too."*

I have often heard it said that what we are seeking in spirituality and spiritual practice is 'happiness.' If that's so, then sometimes I'm failing miserably, and so are a lot of others. But then again, maybe we are seeking the wrong thing. After all, if the result of spiritual practice is

---

* This article was first published in *Delumin/a. Spirituality. Culture. Arts.*, March 7th, 2018.

supposed to be 'happiness,' then the amount of happiness we feel is the measure of our success on the spiritual path, and many broken-hearted mystics and saints throughout history would have to be accounted spiritual 'failures.'

The truth is, I am not really sure what happiness has to do with spirituality. There is such a thing as 'happiness,' and it is certainly desirable. I have known it and been grateful for it, and will likely know it again. I look for it like everybody else. I have friends that I treasure, people I love, work that is often fulfilling; but am I happy? It's hard to say. I'm not sure that I am. I think the most I can say right now is that I'm in love—with those people, and with the world—but it's *love*, not necessarily *happiness*.

There are so many losses and things broken in life, things we can't fix, that often we 'struggle with living.' Sometimes we're not even sure that we want to live; it is hard to see a way forward, hard to endure the utter impossibility of living with what is simply *'not right'* in the world.

Does that make us spiritual failures? It can feel that way. But maybe there is a more important measure to consider, a more tangible proof of spiritual growth than happiness. I think it is *How we act.*

Whether I am happy or sad, heartbroken or world-weary, can I show up when I am needed? Can I rise above my own sadness to be there for someone else in *their* sadness or trouble? In the midst of my own pain, can I put it aside to meet the need of the moment—to be a "child of the moment," as Rumi suggests.[1] Or will I ignore them in my private despair, fail to see their need while thinking of my own and miss the moment of my own calling?

The proof of spirituality or spiritual maturity is not to be unaffected by the vicissitudes of life, or to achieve some permanently blissful—or alternatively, emotionally aloof—state, but to transcend self-absorption in our own highs and lows when the need arises, when we're called upon to serve others, and the world larger than our own needs.

Those personal needs are important, of course, and we have the right to try to get them met, but not at the expense of another's need in a moment of responsibility, not in forgetfulness of the larger body to which we belong. It may seem paradoxical, but in the end, the happiness we must seek . . . is another's.

The Uses and Abuses of Religion
& Spiritual Leadership Today*

An Interview with Netanel Miles-Yépez

Zachary Amitai Malone: Why do people have so many problems with religion?

Netanel Miles-Yépez: I often hear complaints from people for whom 'religion' is a dirty word. They point to current conflicts in the Middle East and historical conflicts like the Crusades and make sweeping statements like, "Religion is the cause of all wars and hatred between peoples." Or, looking at historical examples and the vestiges of patriarchal oppression in various religions today, they say, "Religions are responsible for subjugating women and other marginalized peoples." And I understand what they are saying and where they are coming from when they say it, but my response is usually to challenge the assumptions underlying these statements. Often I respond, *"But religions don't exist . . .* How can they be responsible for these things?"

Z.A.M.: Meaning that there is no such 'thing' as religion; they're putting the blame on a ghost, an apparition?

---

* An interview conducted in 2012 by Zachary Amitai Malone, originally published in *Spectrum: A Journal of Renewal Spirituality,* June 20th, 2013.

N.M-Y.: Exactly . . . Look around and show me a religion. It's an abstraction, an idea; there is no object to receive the blame. There are only *people*, people who believe they 'belong to a religion,' and who believe that they are acting according to 'its dictates.'

Who is really responsible for the so-called 'crimes' of religion? We need only look in a mirror. We have to start taking responsibility for what we do in the name of religion, and what other human beings have done in the past. You'd be on much surer ground to say, 'Human beings are the cause of all wars and hatred between peoples,' and 'Men have attempted to subjugate women.' Those statements are far less interesting, but at least they're accurate. It's just too easy and convenient to make religion a scapegoat for all the things we do to each other.

Z.A.M.: Essentially, we hide our personal 'shadow' material in a fictional enemy, projecting it onto a paper tiger that we can look good fighting?

N.M-Y.: Yes . . . And many of the abuses we see in religion come from people who are actually using it to execute other agendas. At a certain point in the Middle East, you were more likely to find impassioned Communists than Muslim extremists among the youth, because it was Communism in those years that seemed to be offering them a path to personal and political liberation. That was the agenda; Communism was the means of achieving it. When religion is used to achieve political ends, there is a great danger of abuse.

Z.A.M.: Then is religion in itself neutral?

N.M-Y.: Well, I would say, like anything else, it can be used *effectively* . . . or *misused,* as it often is.

Z.A.M.: As it was misused during the Crusades and other religious wars.

N.M-Y.: One doesn't need to know a lot about adolescent human psychology to know that young men will look for nearly any excuse to 'draw a sword' in an exotic land. The same is true of greedy men, except that they tend to ask the young men to do the dirty work for them.

But how many wars were fought between Catholic Christian kings of European countries? They certainly weren't fighting over religion. And even when they seemed to be, as we saw with the Thirty Years War between Catholics and Protestants, any historian will tell you it had just as much to do with a long-standing Bourbon-Hapsburg rivalry.

The truth is, we had plenty of wars before the ecclesiastical-political ascendency of Christianity and Islam that had little or nothing to do with religion, and two World Wars since. The Nazis considered it 'un-enlightened' to persecute someone over religion; it was 'Semitic' peoples they considered inferior. Was that better?

Z.A.M.: I see; religion is not usually the cause of these conflicts, it is the vehicle. Then maybe we should talk about what religion is in itself and how it should be used. So can you tell me . . . *What is religion?*

N.M-Y.: Religion is a sociological construct meant to take us back to the primary experience from which it arose;

it enshrines an ideal and provides one with a structured approach to spiritual awakening.

Z.A.M.: And how should religions be used?

N.M-Y.: Ideally, according to the definition I have just given. That is to say, with an understanding that the religion is a boat that takes you somewhere, as the Buddha taught. Actually, what he said was that it is like a raft one uses to cross a river; once you are on the other side, you don't need to carry it around on your back![1]

You see, religion should be used by *us* . . . and not the other way around. My teacher, Rabbi Zalman Schachter-Shalomi, sometimes says. "Good religion puts itself in the service of God; bad religion puts God in the service of religion."[2] In the same way, "good religion" should serve the individual trying to get somewhere; it should not try to put the individual "in the service of religion."

When our religious authorities start putting religious adherents in the service of the religion, things begin to go wrong. The focus of religious activity becomes the support of the religious structures and the ecclesiastical authorities, and not the fostering of a primary spiritual experience.

If we take Christianity as an example, the source experience of the path is Jesus' profound realization of *divine relationship,* that he was a 'son of God,' and by following his path, we too might find our own way into the same realization. But if we really want to 'build Jesus up' and *"pedestal-ize"* him, as Alan Watts put it, making Jesus *the* Son of God, not *a* son of God, then his realization becomes something that should not be sought.[3] It would be hubris to think we could achieve the same experience, or worse, heresy. So once we put Jesus on that particular pedestal, then we don't actually want anybody else to achieve the same thing. And if the teaching of Christianity is not meant to link us back to *that* primary experience— in which we learn that we are actually the 'children of God'—then what is it?

Z.A.M.: And in the experience of learning that I am 'a child of God,' I am also led into more universal frames of reference, which is dangerous to religious authority?

N.M-Y.: Very much so. And a religion that takes the source or peak experience 'off the table' needs to offer a penultimate experience to its adherents. Now the best one can do is to have some sort of unifying moment with Jesus himself, as opposed to God.

Z.A.M.: So now experiences are mediated?

N.M-Y.: Yes, the peak primary experience is then mediated. Unifying experiences, or experiences of unification, are potentially dangerous to the religious power structure, so they will want to offer 'safer' primary experiences.

At the upper limit of those safer primary experiences might be confirming visions and auditory experiences of Jesus himself, or of his mother, Mary. At the lower limit, perhaps an inner testimony of the spirit that allows one to invest more faith in the religious structure—enough to say it works; but not enough to challenge any of its conventions.
Z.A.M.: How do we bypass the dysfunction and hierarchy of religions to engage in a primary experience of our own?

N.M-Y.: One doesn't necessarily have to "bypass" religion. If the religion is functioning according to its true purpose, under the leadership of those who understand its function, it can serve a person very well. That is to say, if a religion is leaving a trail of 'breadcrumbs' back to the source experience, or to experiences of greater depth, then there is no need to bypass anything.

But, whether it is functioning well or not, a person always has to take responsibility for their own spiritual path. Remember, you are relating to a social construct that doesn't exist except in you! If you know that, then you know that what *you* do with that religion is most important.

In some ways, a religion is its *magisterium*—the body of associated teachings, traditions and technologies that have come down to us through the centuries. And each *magisterium* presents us with tools and structures that may be used to get somewhere. But we have to take responsibility for using the teachings and technologies available in these *magisteria* to achieve our goals. Our success will depend largely on our own integrity, on our own desires and potentials.

The Teacher-Student Relationship

Z.A.M.: What are the actions for which we should take responsibility?

N.M-Y.: Prayer, ritual, study. We are the 'active ingredient' in the relationship with that which the *magisterium* brings down to us.

Z.A.M.: What is the litmus test for engaging one's spiritual path with integrity? How do we know if we're lining up with our own integrity? How do we know if our primary experiences are trustworthy?

N.M-Y.: Well, often we don't. Often we are 'in the dark' in our own lives, until some situation causes us to realize that we are not doing something according to our own integrity.

It has to be a *realization.* If we didn't fumble around in the dark for a while, we'd never have an appreciation for the clarity that comes with the light. The preliminary ignorance is critical to creating a powerful realization. Even so, we're not always very reliable about knowing whether we're acting with integrity or not. For this reason—because we are so likely to err, and so capable of fooling ourselves about our own motivations—we often need the guidance of a spiritual mentor.

The spiritual mentor or guide is meant to challenge you, to be objective, experienced, mature and intuitive enough, to be able to note when you are acting with integrity or not, to know when you are not challenging yourself, to notice when your excuses seem all too convenient.

Z.A.M.: How do we know if a guide is qualified and trustworthy enough to help us maintain our integrity?

N.M-Y. In the same way trust and understanding are built in any relationship—over time, and through situations that test the relationship. It is said that Swami Vivekananda, the great disciple of Ramakrishna Paramahamsa, tested his master for twelve years![4] Apparently Vivekananda had lingering doubts—he was a rational-scientific type—and yet, knew he was getting something good enough to merit staying in Ramakrishna's orbit through all of those years.

We have to build a kind of inner testimony about the relationship: Do we come away from encounters enhanced or diminished? Are we being helped to integrate our qualities in a way that is more holistic, or are we being divided against ourselves? Are we being encouraged to put the guide on a pedestal, or is the guide working to empower and liberate us from such dependencies?

These are questions to ask and the things to watch. Once again, we have to take responsibility for our own spiritual path. If we seem to be ceding responsibility for it to a teacher, or that teacher seems to be taking over that responsibility, there is something to examine there. It is not necessarily, 'Ah-ha! I see your evil plan now!' But we do have to watch out and be aware of how things are unfolding over time.

Sometimes a spiritual guide has to turn a situation 'on its head' to illustrate a point, but there are also some pretty clear lines that one should be careful of crossing. There are few, if any, situations when a sexual relationship is appropriate between a teacher and student, and the consequences of giving or receiving extraordinary monetary gifts should also be carefully considered.

And these cautions run both ways; it is not just the abuse of power that we have to consider. Sometimes students who are wealthy try to 'buy' spirituality and access to a teacher, or try to use their control of the 'purse strings' as a means of avoiding being challenged. Likewise, some students who are attracted to the charisma of teacher mistakenly see romatic or sexual partnership as a short cut to having all that they want.

Z.A.M.: Interesting, the temptation to offer one's body as a substitute for one's soul.

N.M-Y.: Charisma is magnetic and draws people naturally. Unfortunately, some tend to think that they can go right to the center of the magnetism and have it for themselves.

The Problems of Modern Spirituality

Z.A.M.: What foundations need to be laid for a healthy spirituality in the future?

N.M-Y.: I really feel like the 'success-model' of marketed spirituality we see everywhere today—where spiritual teachers are clearly marketed like 'self-help gurus' or contemporary celebrities—is antithetical to a deeply holistic and healthy spirituality, both for the teachers, and for those who look to them for guidance. This model—built as it is on Western consumerist notions of convenience, and ideas of extraordinary success—is distinctly unhelpful for doing anything meant to reduce the size of the ego to manageable proportions, or to fit one for service to God. In fact, it tends to have precisely the opposite effect.

Recently, someone sent me a quote from the Dalai Lama questioning these success-oriented values. He said something to this effect, "The world doesn't need more successful people; it needs more peacemakers, healers, and lovers of all kinds."[5]

Likewise, the corporate or organizational model used for spiritual communities in the West is also problematic. It may be a practical necessity to organize as a non-profit, but it seems a mistake to run a spiritual community like one. A spiritual community must be an incubator for spiritual transformation, and must also be based on intimacy and shared experience. It is harder to cultivate these things in the organizational model, where one becomes a member by filling out an application and paying dues.

We don't actually need more organization for healthy spirituality; we need more organic connections for doing spiritual work. In so many ways, the traditional structures of communal practice and intimacy offered in Hasidism, Sufism, and the monastic orders of Christianity are still the best organic models. The challenge is how to use them today.

Z.A.M.: Are you suggesting we need to go back to the communal practice structures of the past?

N.M-Y.: No . . . I'm suggesting we explore ways in which they can be adapted to the present.

We don't need to be contrarian or anti-modernist just because we feel there are problems with modern forms of spirituality. We can't afford to avoid everything associated with the 'success-model' or the 'corporate-organizational models' out there either. We can't afford to say, *'They* are using those technologies, so *we're* gonna' avoid them.' We have modern problems to solve, and we need to work within modernity. But we can't afford to sever our relationship with the Earth either, or those more organic structures that served us so well in the past.

There was a time in the early-to-mid 20th-century when every block in Warsaw had its own *rebbe,* a Hasidic master who led a community of neighborhood Hasidim. I assume there was a similar situation among the Sufis of Istanbul as well. But today, we tend to have community connections with people who live in widely disparate places. So the question is: How can we keep up the contact and intimacy of the old local communities, as they once existed in Warsaw and Istanbul, in our non-local communities of today? After all, our heart-connections are not less profound because we are physically separated from one another. And how can we not embrace one another as 'community,' even if distant, knowing the rarity of such affinities? We have to use the available technologies that make this possible, to maintain and enhance the intimacy between us, and to exploit them as vehicles for spiritual guidance.

Spiritual Guidance and Community

Z.A.M.: What of the tele-courses and video lectures that are so popular today? Often, the only guidance some spiritual practitioners receive is through recorded media.

N.M-Y.: Well, part of me wants to say, 'It's better than nothing.' But the other part knows it is inferior to direct, one-on-one spiritual guidance, and being present to one another in real-time. It's not wrong, but it is clearly a stop-gap measure. It's not easy to make that situation work for deep spiritual transformation. How is the teacher's unique mirroring challenge to a student offered in that situation?

Now someone might say, 'Every time I hear that talk I feel challenged.' That's good, and I know what they are talking about, having experienced it myself. But there are also major limitations and loopholes. The challenge is not alive and demanding a response in the same way it would be if it were being directed at you from a teacher working from intuition. The only challenge you feel in the former situation is the one you *allow* yourself to feel. What about the challenge to those things you can't see, that you are blind to?

In the end, learning from a video talk is not much different from trying to learn spirituality from a book; both are wonderful vehicles for information; but much of the nuance and subtlety is learned in relationship.

Z.A.M.: In that informational context, one's conscience is allowed more flexibility than in the direct situation of one-on-one confrontation, where one's ego may get squeezed a bit.

N.M-Y.: Yes . . . Two people actually interacting face-to-face, in the same space and time, is not a 'technology' we can afford to leave behind. It's too bad that we don't have porches anymore upon which we could sit in the evenings and interact with our neighbors as we used to. Our intense focus on isolating media is a problem for us. In fact, I tend to think that our increasing isolation is among the biggest dangers facing humanity today.

Z.A.M.: And yet, we're more technologically plugged-in and talk more than ever.

N.M-Y.: That's the paradox: we talk *more* and say *less* than ever, on our phones, on social media, in opinion posts. There is a lot of mind-chatter out there, reporting of ordinary daily activities and dropping half- and entirely un-considered opinions. The challenge is to use the same technology to facilitate intimacy, to communicate at depth, and to convey more valuable information for a community of spiritual seekers.

Z.A.M.: Why is it so difficult to find that intimacy in a group setting today?

N.M-Y.: Akiva Ernst Simon, a professor at the Hebrew University in the 20th-century and a student of Martin Buber said, "The people I can talk to, I can't pray with; and the people I can pray with, I can't talk to."[6] It's difficult to find people with whom you can do both today, at least for some of us.

What we are looking for is more overlap with people, people who are different, and yet share enough with us to make us feel safe and more understood. Such communities have always been intimacy-based communities, as opposed to membership communities. With intimacy, you can be different; there can be love for one another without necessarily liking one another. But community members without an experience of intimacy are just people in a room together.

The Geologist of the Soul

Z.A.M.: How does this relate to the idea of the *neshamah k'lalit* in Hasidism?

N.M-Y.: Neshamah k'lalit means 'aggregate' or 'general soul.' We can look at this in two ways. From one perspective, the *rebbe*, or spiritual master, is a 'general soul.' What makes that person a general soul? The fact that they can address the needs of many different kinds of souls. It is as if they are a 'universal outlet'—lots of people can come and plug into them and receive what they need. People that can only relate to one type of person are not general souls. Those who cannot find compassion for a broad group of people cannot be spiritual leaders. One can be very smart, a spiritual genius or a great spiritual practitioner, and still not be a *neshamah k'lalit* or general soul. So, that's the *neshamah k'lalit* as an individual.

But the *neshamah k'lalit* is also understood as an 'aggregate soul,' made up of many parts, many people sharing a greater soul. Imagine a crowd of people standing in a circle in a small room, all of them reaching one arm toward the center. The part of each person that is reaching for the center is part of an aggregate soul, reaching for the same thing—*the center.* Each person remains an individual, but they are all connected by their desire for the 'center.'

Now, the leader of the group, the 'general soul,' is often symbolic of the group itself and its center, but is not *actually* the center. The leader is only functioning to form connections for the group. Think of it this way: During the 2008 presidential campaign, Barack Obama was going around the country, from city to city, saying—"Yes we can!" And everywhere he went, he got other people to say that with him; he was actually building that *"We."* That is to say, all the people who invested in that idea became that *We.* Unfortunately, many of them forgot the message—"Yes *we* can!"—while staring at the messenger, and thus were disappointed when he wasn't able to do it all by himself, without them.

He was the symbol and the one who helped to create the connections. That is the function of the spiritual leader; but if we forget that a person in this position is just the symbol and facilitator, we are often disappointed with what has not been achieved.

Z.A.M.: I know you are familiar with the metaphor of the 'Geologist of the Soul.' Can you tell me what this means to you?

N.M-Y.: I have always loved this *mashal*, this 'analogy,' which my teacher Rabbi Zalman Schachter-Shalomi heard directly from his own *rebbe*, Rabbi Menachem Mendel Schneerson, the seventh Lubavitcher Rebbe.

First of all, when the Rebbe was challenged with the question, "What is a *rebbe* good for?" He says, "I can't speak about myself; but I'll talk about my own *rebbe*," Rabbi Yosef Yitzhak Schneersohn, the sixth Lubavitcher Rebbe. Then he goes on to tell us that a *rebbe* can help you locate what is most precious inside you—"gold, and silver, and diamonds." And in as much as they do that, they are valuable to you. But they are not themselves the focus; they are helping you to find the focus, which is the divinity within you.[7]

This is really the model and the metaphor for spiritual leadership that we need to use in the emerging paradigm. We need to look at our spiritual teachers from this perspective: in as much as they help me find that 'inner treasure,' that thing that is most precious within me, they are serving their purpose and fulfilling their function, but they are not the focus of my spiritual path. The goal of the spiritual path is not to make an idol out of the spiritual guide, nor is it to become a spiritual leader or guide oneself. That is a vocation and a function. The goal is the inner discovery of divinity! Not everybody is a general soul in this way, nor do they need to be. It's a job, and not always a pleasant one. The guide is a mirror.

Z.A.M.: How does the spiritual guide, the 'Geologist of the Soul,' get to know where this 'gold' is?

N.M-Y.: That is an important question. The 'Geologist of the Soul,' like any good geologist, has to have studied and spent time in the 'lab,' and most importantly, done their own 'fieldwork.' The Geologist of the Soul draws upon both knowledge and intuition in the context of experience to say where the 'gold' is. The geologist knows because they have *been there*, because they have actually found some of that precious treasure, and knows how to read the signs.

But I also want to say that it is not good for a spiritual guide to rest on their laurels. It is easy to get distracted by the vocation and its demands, to get caught up in the role and identifying with the role. That's why I was so delighted when I first learned Shaykh Shahab ad-Din Suhrawardi's guidance on being a Sufi *shaykh*. It says nothing about *status;* it is all about *responsibility.* And among the shaykh's chief responsibilities is to keep up with and maintain their own spiritual practice.

It is very easy to get distracted from those practices when you are leading others. Often, it's unavoidable. Leading others *does* distract you from doing that work, and sometimes you even want to escape so that you can do it again. But if it ever becomes an excuse, then you've got a problem to deal with. You have to keep trying to cultivate your own spiritual life. That's the burden Suhrawardi lays on us: You cannot quit trying, because these are the terms of your empowerment, and that's important.

Z.A.M.: So the 'Geologist of the Soul' has to have both deep experience and a continuing commitment to cultivating more experience.

N.M-Y.: The Geologist of the Soul has to be mature and experienced enough, to be deeply connected enough to be able to witness how the spiritual path tends to work. They have to have had experiences that they can speak to, that are regular enough that they can be conveyed in principle to another with the words: 'Here's what to look for . . . Here's how you will trick yourself . . . I've been around that corner myself . . . Here's what you're likely to find.'

Z.A.M.: Do degrees of spiritual experience and depth make a difference?

N.M-Y.: The more mature the practitioner, the more experience they have, the more they can say. The less mature, with less experience, the less they can say. Nevertheless, they still may be able to say something, and that too is helpful. Anybody who has more experience than you, and with whom you have a good connection, can give you some good advice. Not every mentor or guide has to be a master on "the 20th plane."[8] But the connection needs to be good, and there does need to be a respect for the law of gravity, meaning that there is an attraction between the two of you, and just as with gravity, some things have to come down.

Z.A.M.: You mean there is a necessary element of hierarchy?

N.M-Y.: It's just gravity. Let me tell you one of my favorite Hasidic anecdotes. It's about a Hasidic master named Reb Moshe of Kobrin. One day, he's out for a walk in the woods and runs into one of his old schoolfellows. His old buddy stops him and says, "Oh, Reb Moshe! It's so good to see you! I heard that you're a *rebbe* now?" Reb Moshe shrugs his shoulders. His friend says: "I want to ask you a serious question. At this point in my life, I need to make some changes. My life is not where I would like it to be, and I've heard how you help people now. The problem is, I remember what you were like as a kid. I remember the things you did—the things we did together! So what I need to know is this: what do I need to believe about you in order to have the benefit of your guidance?"

As Jesus says, "A prophet is not without honor except in their own land."[9] Because people remember what you were like as a kid—maybe you were not very confident, or maybe you were a bully, or a prankster. So this guy knows Reb Moshe's past and asks a very intelligent question. He is saying: 'I have memories of these things, and I'm not going to lose them so easily. When I look at you, I remember who you used to be. And yet, I also believe that maybe you've changed, because people come to you for help and seem helped by you. Now *I* need some help; so what do *I* need to believe about *you* in order to get that help?'

Reb Moshe shakes his head for a moment, thinking. He looks around and sees a tree stump, walks over to it and hops up on it, saying: "This is as much as you need to believe. You don't need to believe that I'm sitting on top of that tall tree over there, surveying the landscape for miles around. But you do have to believe that I'm at least on top of this tree stump, just a foot or two higher than you; because, from up here, I can see just a little farther. And that's enough to help."

Z.A.M.: From there he can offer just a little more perspective.

N.M-Y.: I think it's really a great way to look at spiritual leadership. If we are walking down the street, and I'm walking just ahead of you, and I turn a corner before you, I'm in a position to tell you what's around that corner, if there is something dangerous there. It's as simple as that.

There are all kinds of mentors available to us, and that's as much as we need to believe about them. We don't have to make idols out of them. In some ways, making idols out of them renders them useless to us as accessible models. It leads us to believe we can never reach their level. And we tend to give away responsibility to them. After all, they look so high—and we help build them up so high—that we know we can never get there ourselves . . . *and we stop trying.* We say, 'Oh, they'll do the work for me.'

Or, the other problem is that *we* want to be on top of the tree and have some sort of status or identity built around that. The tree stump model is much more useful, and most of the time, just truer.

Notes

Preface

1. Wilfred Cantwell Smith, *The Meaning and End of Religion*, New York, NY: The New American Library, 1964: 7.

Epochs & Reality Maps

1. 'Epochs' and 'reality maps' are terms and themes taken over from my teacher Zalman Schachter-Shalomi, which I desired to give a more thorough description. See Zalman Schachter-Shalomi, *Paradigm Shift: From the Jewish Renewal Teachings of Reb Zalman Schachter-Shalomi*, ed. Ellen Singer, Northvale, NJ: Jason Aronson, Inc., 1993: 287-290, 299-307.

2. Lawrence Weschler, *Seeing is Forgetting the Name of the Thing One Sees: A Life of Contemporary Artist Robert Irwin*, Berkeley, California: University of California Press, 1982: 201.

The End of Religion

1. P. D. Ouspensky, *The Symbolism of the Tarot: Philosophy of Occultism in Pictures and Numbers*, tr. A. L. Pogossky, New York: Dover Publications, 1976: 48-49.

2. "The Raft Simile" in the Pali *Alagaddupama Sutta*.

3. Heard directly from Schachter-Shalomi after giving a Yom Kippur sermon at Makom Ohr Shalom in Los Angeles, California, in which he used this formulation for the first time, ca. 2009.

Spiritual and *Religious*

1. *The New Testament,* The Gospel of Luke 10:42.

2. Netanel Miles-Yépez and Zalman Schachter-Shalomi, *God Hidden, Whereabouts Unknown: The Holy Ari and the 'Contraction' of God: Third Expanded Edition,* Boulder, CO: Albion-Andalus Books, 2021: 32.

3. Friedrich Nietzsche, *The Gay Science,* tr. Walter Kaufmann, New York: Vintage, 1974: 181.

The Religion of Spirituality

1. Max Zeller, *The Dream: The Vision of the Night,* ed. Janet Dallett, Los Angeles: The Analytical Psychology Club of Los Angeles, 1975:2.

2. Actually, the 'tree of the knowledge of good and evil,' *etz hada'at tov va-ra,* Genesis 2-3.

3. After similar usage by Zalman Schachter-Shalomi, who often referred to the hyphen connecting a person to more than one religious commitment.

4. A phrase used by philosopher Ken Wilber in his descriptions of holarchies.

5. Zeller, *The Dream,* 2.

*The Snowmass Conference
& the True Heart of Dialogue*

1. Netanel Miles-Yepez, ed., *The Common Heart: An Experience of Interreligious Dialogue,* New York: Lantern Books, 2006: 3.

2. Miles-Yepez, *The Common Heart*, 34.

3. Ibid, 16.

Paradigms of Ecumenism
as a Spiritual Practice

1. This was the Spiritual Paths Foundation's "Way of Contemplation" seminar in Aspen, Colorado (August 23–25th, 2002). Its speakers included Father Thomas Keating, Rabbi Rami Shapiro, Imam Feisal Abdul-Rauf, Swami Atmarupananda, Ajahn Sundara, and Dr. Edward W. Bastian. This culminated in the small book, N. Miles-Yépez, ed., *The Way of Contemplation and Meditation*, Woody Creek, CO: Spiritual Paths Publishing, 2002.

2. Matthew Fox, *One River, Many Wells: Wisdom Springing from Global Faiths*, New York, NY: Jeremy P. Tarcher/Putnam, 2000: 4-5.

3. Often heard directly from Zalman Schachter-Shalomi.

4. This is actually an oft-quoted paraphrase of Müller, who merely applied Goethe's "He who knows one, knows none" to religion. F. Max Müller, *Introduction to the Science of Religion*, London: Longmans, Green, and Co., 1882: 13.

5. Netanel Miles-Yépez, ed., *The Common Heart: An Experience of Interreligious Dialogue: The Snowmass Interreligious Conference Reflects on Twenty Years of Dialogue*. New York: Lantern Books, 2006.

6. Raimundo Panikkar, ed., *Blessed Simplicity: The Monk as Universal Archetype*. New York: Seabury Press, 1982.

7. Christopher Isherwood, ed., *Vedanta for the Western World: Vedanta and the West*. London: Allen & Unwin; Hollywood, CA: Vedanta press, 1951.

8. Thomas Keating, *Crisis of Faith, Crisis of Love*. New York: Continuum, 1995.

9. Jacob Needleman, *Lost Christianity: A Journey of Rediscovery to the Centre of Christian Experience*, New York, NY: Doubleday & Company, Inc., 1980.

10. The final version of these points may be found in Miles-Yépez, *The Common Heart*, xvii–xix.

11. Isherwood, *Vedanta for the Western World*, 1951.

12. Paraphrase of Raimundo Panikkar in *Art Meets Spirituality in a Changing Economy: The Shifting Paradigm*, Mystic Fire Video, 1998.

13. See Ken Wilber, *The Collected Works of Ken Wilber: Volume VII: A Brief History of Everything, The Eye of the Spirit*, Boston, MA: Shambhala Publications, 2000: 40-41 note 12, 276-279.

Courage, Interreligious Dialogue, and Engaged Buddhism

1. W. Y. Evans-Wentz, ed., *The Tibetan Book of the Great Liberation: or, The Method of Realizing Nirvana Through Knowing the Mind Preceded by an Epitome of Padma-Sambhava's Biography and Followed by Guru Phadampa Sangay's Teachings. According to English renderings by Sardar Bahādur S. W. Laden La and by the Lāmas Karma Sumdhon Paul, Lobzang Mingyur Dorje, and Kazi Dawa-Samdup*, London/New York, NY: Oxford University Press, 1954.

Foundations of the Fourth Turning of Hasidism

1. In speaking of 'turnings,' Zalman Schachter-Shalomi and I are consciously borrowing language from the Buddhist tradition, which speaks of 'three turnings of the wheel of

dharma,' describing three phases of how the wisdom of that tradition was presented according to the needs of different eras.

2. Chthonic (from the Greek word, *chthon* or 'earth') referring to how the land itself, or the landscape of a place influences expression in that place.

3. The expression *hasidim ha'rishonim* may be read both ways. It occurs many times in the Mishnah. One example is found in Berakhot 5:1.

4. Another possibility is the Aramaic word, *asyah*, 'healing.'

5. 1 Maccabees 2:42.

6. Philo of Alexandria, *Quod Omnis Probus Liber Sit,* sections XII and XIII.

7. As they are called by Pliny the Elder.

8. Although this group did identify themselves as Ḥasidim, "Ḥasidei Sefarad" is simply a name we have applied to them for the purpose of differentiating them from their northern siblings, the Ḥasidei Ashkenaz.

9. See Zalman Schachter-Shalomi and Netanel Miles-Yépez, *A Heart Afire: Stories and Teachings of the Early Hasidic Masters,* Philadelphia, PA: Jewish Publication Society, 2009: 44-54, and 294-95.

10. See Schachter-Shalomi, *A Heart Afire,* 180-92.

11. From the tri-literal Hebrew root, *Nun-Beit-Beit,* which may be interpreted as 'hollow.'

12. *Davvenen* may be derived from the Latin word, *divinum,* meaning, 'divine work.'

13. See Schachter-Shalomi, *A Heart Afire,* 306-31.

14. See Zalman Schachter-Shalomi and Netanel Miles-Yépez, *A Hidden Light: Stories and Teachings of Early HaBaD and Bratzlav Hasidism*, Santa Fe, NM: Gaon Books, 2011: 160.

15. See Schachter-Shalomi, *A Heart Afire*, 26-44.

16. Another term for what we have sometimes called 'paradigm shift,' a phrase originally introduced by the philosopher of science, Thomas Kuhn.

17. We have borrowed the term 'deep structures' from Noam Chomsky's discussion of transformational grammar.

18. 'Deep ecumenism' is a phrase coined by Father Matthew Fox. Ecumenism, from the Greek, *oikoumenikos,* 'from the whole world,' originally referred to cooperative efforts between different parts of the Christian Church.

A Rebbe's Soul, A Hasid's Yearning

1. Zalman Schachter-Shalomi and Netanel Miles-Yépez, *A Heart Afire: Stories and Teachings of the Early Hasidic Masters,* Philadelphia: Jewish Publication Society, 2009: 252-53.

2. See Zalman Schachter-Shalomi, *A Heart Afire*, 295.

3. Ibid., 158-61.

4. This dialogue was published in Zalman Schachter-Shalomi, *The Geologist of the Soul: Talks on Rebbe-craft and Spiritual Leadership,* ed. N.M-Y., Boulder, CO: Albion-Andlaus Books, 2012.

5. See Zalman Schachter-Shalomi, *A Heart Afire*, 187.

6. See Zalman Schachter-Shalomi and Netanel Miles-Yépez, *A Hidden Light: Stories and Teachings of Early HaBaD and Bratzlav Hasidism*, Santa Fe, NM: Gaon Books, 2011: 160.

7. Dir. Vikram Gandhi. *Kumaré.* Kino Lorber, 2011.

8. See Martin Buber, *Tales of the Hasidim: The Early Masters*, tr. Olga Marx, New York, NY: Schocken Books, 1947: 54-55.

9. Zalman Schachter-Shalomi, *Wrapped in a Holy Flame: Teachings and Tales of the Hasidic Masters*, ed. N. Miles-Yépez, San Francisco, CA: Jossey-Bass, 2003: 65-66.

Matisyahu & The New T'shuvah

1. See Zalman Schachter-Shalomi and Netanel Miles-Yépez, *A Hidden Light: Stories and Teachings of Early HaBaD and Bratzlav Hasidism*, Santa Fe, NM: Gaon Books, 2011: 315-20.

2. Abraham Schischa, "Kalev, Yitzhak Eizig, of Nagys-zollos," *The Encyclopedia of Hasidism*, ed. Tzvi M. Rabinowicz, Northvale, NJ: Jason Aronson, Inc., 1996.

3. See Matthew Perpetua, "Matisyahu Shaves Off His Trademark Beard," *Rolling Stone*, December 14th, 2011, and Cara Kelly, "Matisyahu Shaves Beard, Leaves Fans Confused," December 15th, 2011.

4. Quote attributed to Mohandas K. Gandhi.

The Miracle of Re-Dedication

1. The original article referenced both Hurricane Sandy and victims of missile strikes in Israel. In Judaism, a *d'rash* is a teaching or interpretation.

2. The question is: Is it better to light the *menorah* right away, returning God's light to the Temple immediately, even if it is only for one day? Or, should they wait the eight days it would take to make new oil so that the *menorah* would not go out again? In the end, they decided it was better to return God's light to the Temple immediately, to make things right as soon as

possible. And this decision led to the miracle of Ḥannukah—for the oil that should have only lasted a day actually lasted the entire eight days it took to make new oil!

3. Each night, another candle is added to the eight-branched *menorah*, thus emphasizing the increaing miracle of how the single cruse of oil continued to burn.

The Other Side of Fear

1. William Shakespeare, *Julius Caesar*, Act 1, Scene 2.

What's Happiness Got To Do With It?

1. See Annemarie Schimmel, *Mystical Dimensions of Islam*, Chapel Hill, NC: University of North Carolina Press, 1975: 130.

The Uses and Abuses of Religion
& Spiritual Leadership Today

1. "The Raft Simile" in the Pali *Alagaddupama Sutta*.

2. Heard directly from Schachter-Shalomi after giving a Yom Kippur sermon at Makom Ohr Shalom in Los Angeles, California, in which he used this formulation for the first time, ca. 2009.

3. Audio lecture by Alan Watts, "Jesus, His Religion," *Myth and Religion*, Alan Watts Organization.

4. A commonly repeated anecdote in the Vedanta tradition.

5. A quote commonly attributed to the 14th Dalai Lama, Tenzin Gyatso.

6. Quote commonly attributed to Akiva Ernst Simon.

7. Zalman Schachter-Shalomi, *The Geologist of the Soul: Talks on Rebbe-craft and Spiritual Leadership*, ed. N.M-Y., Boulder, CO: Albion-Andlaus Books, 2012: xi.

8. A medium named Agnes Taylor reported to Rabbi Zalman Schachter-Shalomi that his *rebbe*, Rabbi Yosef Yitzhak Schneersohn was visiting from "the 20th plane." Heard directly from Zalman Schachter-Shalomi.

9. *The New Testament*, Matthew 13:57.

Bibliography

Buber, Martin. *Tales of the Hasidim: The Early Masters.* Tr. Olga Marx. New York, NY: Schocken Books, 1947.

Evans-Wentz, W. Y. ed.. *The Tibetan Book of the Great Liberation: or, The Method of Realizing Nirvana Through Knowing the Mind Preceded by an Epitome of Padma-Sambhava's Biography and Followed by Guru Phadampa Sangay's Teachings According to English renderings by Sardar Bahädur S. W. Laden La and by the Lāmas Karma Sumdhon Paul, Lobzang Mingyur Dorje, and Kazi Dawa-Samdup,* London/New York, NY: Oxford University Press, 1954.

Fox, Matthew. *One River, Many Wells: Wisdom Springing from Global Faiths.* New York, NY: Jeremy P. Tarcher/Putnam, 2000.

Isherwood, Christopher, ed.. *Vedanta for the Western World: Vedanta and the West.* London: Allen & Unwin; Hollywood, CA: Vedanta press, 1951.

Keating, Thomas. *Crisis of Faith, Crisis of Love.* New York: Continuum, 1995.

Kelly, Cara. "Matisyahu Shaves Beard, Leaves Fans Confused." *The Washington Post* (December 15th, 2011).

Malone, Zachary Amitai. "The Uses and Abuses of Religion and Spiritual Leadership: An Interview with Netanel Miles-Yépez." *Spectrum: A Journal of Renewal Spirituality.* June 20, 2013. Online Edition.

Matisyahu and Netanel Miles-Yépez. "The Hanukkah Miracle of Re-Dedication." *The Huffington Post.* December 10, 2012. Online Edition.

Miles-Yépez, N., ed.. *The Way of Contemplation and Meditation.* Woody Creek, CO: Spiritual Paths Publishing, 2002.

Miles-Yépez, Netanel. "Courage, Inter-Spiritual Dialogue & Engaged Buddhism: An Interview with Tania Leontov." *Spectrum: A Jouranl of Renewal Spirituality* (Volume 3; Number 2, 2007). Online Edition.

——. "The End of Religion," *The Huffington Post.* March 3, 2014. Online Edition.

——. "Matisyahu and the New T'shuvah." *Spectrum: A Journal of Renewal Spirituality.* September 6, 2012. Online Edition.

——. "The Other Side of Fear." *Spectrum: A Journal of Renewal Spirituality.* August 25, 2013. Online Edition.

——. "Paradigms of Ecumenism as a Spiritual Practice: Father Thomas Keating and Swami Atmarupananda Discuss the Theory and Practice of Dialogue." *Journal of Ecumenical Studies* (Vol. 43, No. 1, Winter 2008).

——. "The Religion of Spirituality. *The Huffington Post.* August 12, 2014. Online Edition.

——. "The Snowmass Conference and the True Heart of Dialogue." *Spectrum: A Jouranl of Renewal Spirituality: Volume 2; Number 1, Winter-Spring 2006.* Boulder, CO: Albion-Andalus Books, 2019.

——. "Spiritual *and* Religious." *The Huffington Post.* March 3, 2014. Online Edition.

——. "What's Happiness Got to Do With It?" *Delumin/a. Spirituality. Culture. Arts.,* March 7, 2018. Online Edition.

Miles-Yépez, Netanel, ed.. *The Common Heart: An Experience of Interreligious Dialogue.* New York: Lantern Books, 2006.

Miles-Yépez, Netanel, and Zalman Schachter-Shalomi. *Foundations of a Fourth Turning of Hasidism: A Manifesto.* Boulder, CO: Albion-Andalus Books, 2014.

——. *God Hidden, Whereabouts Unknown: The Holy Ari and the 'Contraction' of God: Third Expanded Edition.* Boulder, CO: Albion-Andalus Books, 2021.

Bibliography

Müller, F. Max. *Introduction to the Science of Religion*. London: Longmans, Green, and Co., 1882.

Needleman, Jacob. *Lost Christianity: A Journey of Rediscovery to the Centre of Christian Experience*. New York, NY: Doubleday & Company, Inc., 1980.

Nietzsche, Friedrich. *The Gay Science*. Tr. Walter Kaufmann. New York: Vintage, 1974.

Ouspensky, P. D. *The Symbolism of the Tarot: Philosophy of Occultism in Pictures and Numbers*. Tr. A. L. Pogossky. New York: Dover Publications, 1976.

Panikkar, Raimundo, ed.. *Blessed Simplicity: The Monk as Universal Archetype*. New York: Seabury Press, 1982.

Perpetua, Matthew. "Matisyahu Shaves Off His Trademark Beard." *Rolling Stone* (December 14th, 2011).

Prabhavananda, Swami, and Christopher Isherwood. Tr. *The Song of God: Bhagavad-Gita*. New York: Mentor, 1972.

Schachter-Shalomi, Zalman. *The Geologist of the Soul: Talks on Rebbe-craft and Spiritual Leadership*. Ed. N.M-Y.. Boulder, CO: Albion-Andlaus Books, 2012.

—. *Paradigm Shift: From the Jewish Renewal Teachings of Reb Zalman Schachter-Shalomi*. Ed. Ellen Singer. Northvale, NJ: Jason Aronson, Inc., 1993.

—. *Wrapped in a Holy Flame: Teachings and Tales of the Hasidic Masters*, ed. N. Miles-Yépez, San Francisco, CA: Jossey-Bass, 2003.

Schachter-Shalomi, Zalman, and Netanel Miles-Yépez. "God Hidden, Whereabouts Unknown: Variations on a Kabbalistic Theme (Part I of II)," *Spectrum: A Journal of Renewal Spirituality: Volume 2; Number 1, Winter-Spring 2006*. Boulder, CO: Albion-Andalus Books, 2019: 11-30.

—. *A Heart Afire: Stories and Teachings of the Early Hasidic Masters*. Philadelphia, PA: Jewish Publication Society, 2009.

—. *A Hidden Light: Stories and Teachings of Early HaBaD and Bratzlav Hasidism*, Santa Fe, NM: Gaon Books, 2011.

Schimmel, Annemarie. *Mystical Dimensions of Islam.* Chapel Hill, NC: University of North Carolina Press, 1975.

Schischa, Abraham. "Kalev, Yitzhak Eizig, of Nagys-zollos." *The Encyclopedia of Hasidism.* Ed. Tzvi M. Rabinowicz. Northvale, NJ: Jason Aronson, Inc., 1996.

Smith, Wilfred Cantwell. *The Meaning and End of Religion.* New York, NY: The New American Library, 1964.

Weschler, Lawrence. *Seeing is Forgetting the Name of the Thing One Sees: A Life of Contemporary Artist Robert Irwin.* Berkeley, California: University of California Press, 1982.

Wilber, Ken. *The Collected Works of Ken Wilber: Volume VII: A Brief History of Everything, The Eye of the Spirit.* Boston, MA: Shambhala Publications, 2000.

Zeller, Max. *The Dream: The Vision of the Night.* Ed. Janet Dallett, Los Angeles: The Analytical Psychology Club of Los Angeles, 1975.

Index

Abhishiktananda, Swami (1910-1973), 44

Adam Kadmon, 22

Akong, Rinpoche (1940-2013), 75

America Hurrah (play), 73, 75

Apter Rav (Avraham Yehoshua Heschel, 1748-1825), 107

Archdiocese of Los Angeles, 63

Atmarupananda, Swami, x, xvi, 33, 36-38, 55-70, 175

avodat Ha'Shem, 98

Ba'al Shem Tov (Yisrael ben Eliezer, 1698-1760), 98, 101, 107, 108, 116, 117, 120, 127, 128

Bastian, Edward W., ix, xv, 64, 175

Bendictines, 40-41, 85

Benjamin, Terry, 87

Beru, Sherab Palden (1911-2012), 75

bhakti devotionalism, 121

Bielecki, Tessa, x, 77

Blessed Simplicity (book), 41

Bluzhover Rebbe, 112

bodhisattva, 62, 72, 86, 88

Bratzlav Hasidism, 122, 123, 126, 127

Brother Lawrence (ca. 1614-1691), 60

Buber, Martin (1878-1965), 165

Buddha, 11, 22, 156

Index

Sefer Ḥasidim (book), 95

sesshin, 42

Shake Off the Dust... Arise (album), 127

Shakespeare, William (ca. 1585-1613), 138

Shambhala Center, 86, 87

shammes, 117

Shapiro, Rami, 29, 79, 175

Sharon, Jim, xvii

Shekhinah, 123

Shimano, Eido (1932-2018), 44

Shiva Nataraja, 141

shoresh ha'neshamah, 106

shtetl, 120

simḥah, 121

Simhah Bunim (of P'shyskha, ca. 1765-1827), 111

Simmer-Brown, Judith, 77

Simon, Akiva Ernst (1900-1988), 165

Simpson, Eliya, 116

Snowmass Interreligious Conference, x, xv-xvi, 27-32, 36-38, 49-55, 63-70, 72, 77-86, 87

Soen Sa Nim (1927-2004), 49

Spark Seeker (album), 119, 126

spiritual-but-not-religious, 13, 15, 16, 21

Spiritual Paths Foundation, ix, 64, 175

spirituality, xiii, xv, 11, 12, 13-16, 17-23, 40, 45, 46, 51, 57, 63, 72, 85, 94, 109, 115, 120, 121, 122, 124, 149, 150, 161-63, 164

Netanel Miles-Yépez is an artist, philosopher, religion scholar, and spiritual teacher. He is the current head of the Inayati-Maimuni lineage of Sufism, and is considered a leading thinker in the Interspiritual and New Monasticism movements.

Netanel studied History of Religions at Michigan State University and Contemplative Religion at the Naropa Institute, before pursuing traditional studies with such spiritual luminaries as Rabbi Zalman Schachter-Shalomi, founder of the Jewish Renewal movement, and Father Thomas Keating, founder of Contemplative Outreach.

He is the author of *In the Teahouse of Experience: Nine Talks on the Path of Sufism* (2020), *The Merging of Two Oceans: Nine Talks on Sufism & Hasidism* (2021), and the translator of *My Love Stands Behind a Wall: A Translation of the Song of Songs and Other Poems* (2015).

Currently, Netanel lives in Boulder, Colorado, where he is Chair of Religious Studies and Director of the Keating-Schachter Center for Interspirituality at Naropa University, a project of Charis Foundation (charisinterspirituality.org).

www.ingramcontent.com/pod-product-compliance
Lightning Source LLC
Chambersburg PA
CBHW020449130626
46549CB00001B/357